Volume I

ALL CHILDREN CREATE:

LEVELS 1-3

Paula D. Sefkow
Helen L. Berger

AN

ELEMENTARY ART CURRICULUM

Lp Learning Publications, Inc.

Library of Congress Number: 80-82018

Copyright 1981   Paula D. Sefkow and Helen L. Berger

Co-Editors:
  Edsel L. Erickson
  Lois A. Carl

Learning Publications, Inc.
PO Box 1326
Holmes Beach, Florida 33509

ISBN 0-918452-24-4

Cover by Rob Gutek, Aries Graphics

Printing: 4 5 6   Year: 7 8
Printed and bound in the United States of America

ACKNOWLEDGEMENTS

Our special thanks to our principal, teachers, and students at the Parkers Prairie Elementary School, Parkers Prairie, Minnesota. They participated in the field test of this book and made many valuable suggestions.

Dedicated to Dr. Gerald Korte,
in whose inspiring classroom the
idea for this book was conceived.

FOREWORD

This volume of ALL CHILDREN CREATE provides an integrated and comprehensive curriculum of the elements and techniques of art for school levels one through three. It advances and reviews at each succeeding level so that learning is reinforced. This book is for art specialists who are designing curricula and providing resources to teachers. It is also for teachers with limited backgrounds in art who need to see the totality of a coherent art curriculum and have lesson plans for each necessary concept.

Another attribute of this art activities book is that it will stimulate both the art specialist and the classroom teacher to create their own projects within an integrated plan. The teacher may also expand upon or use each lesson as presented.

Art is important to students because it allows them to see with eyes that are more aware. Each lesson allows students to create original work. This broadens their horizons and enhances the world around them making the world appear more interesting, exciting and stimulating.

TABLE OF CONTENTS

TABLE OF CONTENTS

Lessons, Level 2

TABLE OF CONTENTS

Lessons, Level 3

INTRODUCTION

Curriculum Scope and Sequence

General Suggestions

Special Art Supplies

Curriculum Scope and Sequence
Levels 1-3

	LEVEL 1	LEVEL 2	LEVEL 3
ART ELEMENTS	Lesson	Lesson	Lesson
Color:	2, 3	31, 32, 33, 58	61, 62, 75
Line:	22	39	66, 85
Shape:	4, 6, 24	34, 49, 53	63, 79, 86
Texture:	5, 6	37, 54	73
Balance & Symmetry:	16, 24	46, 49	63, 71, 75, 81, 82, 86, 87
TECHNIQUES AND MEDIUMS			
Design:	22, 24, 29, 30	40, 46, 49, 52, 53, 55	63, 66, 71, 82, 86
Drawing & Painting	1, 3, 15, 19, 30	33, 44	67, 68, 76, 83, 84
Watercolor:	14, 26	38, 40	78
Collage	4, 8, 18	32, 37, 57, 58	88
Weaving:	17, 23	48, 54	72, 80
Stitchery	13, 20	41, 59	89
Clay	25	30	65
Sculpture	10, 12, 21, 25	39, 42, 45, 50, 51	69, 73, 81, 85
Printing	9, 27	33, 35, 43	64, 66, 74, 90
Imagination	7, 8	38, 46	70, 82, 84, 90
Group activity	28	55, 56	70
Perspective			77
Special Projects:	11, 15	36, 47	76

General Suggestions

Try each project before presenting the lesson to the class. In this way you will have a better appreciation of the problems students may encounter as well as having an example to show them.

―――――

Use glue, not paste. If a project is important enough for students to spend time on, the results should hold up. Paste very often comes undone before students get their work home.

―――――

Exemplars or illustrations are suggested at the end of many lessons. The student, having worked on a similar project, then has a point of reference which makes the exemplars meaningful. A discussion based on the exemplars acts as a review of the lesson and further increases a student's awareness.

―――――

Student's work should often be displayed. Students learn by seeing how others approach and solve an art problem.

―――――

In exploratory lessons, students should be encouraged to investigate as many facets of the medium as they can rather than being concerned with a finished product.

―――――

Students imagination and creativity are stimulated by interesting surroundings. Walks to experience art concepts in the real world expand the classroom walls. In the classroom a teacher should display materials such as:

> Pictures
> Mounted birds or animals (possibly borrowed from the high school science department)
> Gourds, squash, and Indian corn in the fall.
> Pottery
> Baskets
> Travel posters
> A prism
> Old coffee pots, pitchers, duck decoys, or any other memorabilia of early America
> Folk dolls in foreign costumes
> Vase of weeds

The National Geographic Magazine is an outstanding source of colored photographs for both display and art project use. Copies that can be cut up are invaluable in the classroom.

General Suggestions (continued)

Suggested subjects for paintings are listed below:

Life Under the Sea
Make Believe World
Prehistoric Monsters
Someone I Know
Circus
Big City at Night
Downtown Section of our City
A City Is _____
My Room
Scenes on Other Planets
Fire
Imaginary Animals
Clown
A Bird Tree - with many kinds of birds
Shopping in a Grocery Store
Farm
Jungle
Storm
Sailing Boats
Parade
New York City (What you think it looks like if you've never been there)
Old Tree in Winter
Bridges
On A Picnic
Sports
At a Fair or Carnival
Taking a Trip - Vacation
My Dreams - The Most Exciting Dream I Can Remember
Birthday Party
Wild Animals — tigers, lions, etc.
Football Game
Noah's Ark
Fireworks
Other People in the World
Sunset
Deep in the Forest
Waiting Somewhere
At the Barbers
Big Factory
If I Had A Wish
Treasure Hunt
Masquerade
Camping Out

Special Art Supplies

The following inexpensive items are not usually included with the art supplies provided by schools. You may need to ask your students' parents or your school to provide them.

First Level

Item	Lesson #
Food coloring	2
White frosting	2
Graham crackers	2
Jack-o-lantern lids	9
Boxes and covers	12
Hardware cloth	13
Yarn	13, 20, 23, 26
Boards	15
Wood stain	15
Sandpaper	15, 6
ModPodge	15
Old paint brushes	15
Small calendars	15
Styrofoam meat trays	20, 21
Styrofoam packing material	21
Round toothpicks	21
Blunt pointed darning needles	20
Sides from ½ gallon milk cartons	23
Sponges	27
Pincher clothespins	27

Second Level

Item	Lesson #
Small paper bags	1
Yarn	2, 11, 22, 24, 29
Wallpaper sample book	2
Buttons (purple)	2
Ribbon	2, 24
Pincher clothespins	5
Sponge	5
Aluminum pie tins	5
Wax paper	6
Potato peelers	6, 25
Iron	6
Spray bottles	7
Wire screen	11
Blunt end darning needles	11, 29

Special Art Supplies (continued)

Second Level

Item	Lesson #
Oranges	13
Liquid bleach	14
Q Tips	14
Epsom salts	17
Scrap lumber	20
Material	24
36 mm. color transparency folders	25
Thin, clear, plastic	25
Popsicle sticks	27
Found objects	27
Plastic wrap	28
Burlap	29
Embroidery hoops, small	29
Flour	30
Salt	30
Aluminum foil	30

Third Level

Item	Lesson #
Water soluable clay	5
Dowels	5
Wax paper	5
Small scraps of wood	6, 25
Yarn	9, 21, 29
Aluminum foil	9
Magazine pictures	12
Corn husks	13
Found objects	14
Salad oil	15
Box covers	16
Popsicle sticks	21
Colored, plastic-coated wire	25
Wax paper	27
Potato peeler	27
Burlap	29
10″ embroidery hoops (can be shared by grades 3-6)	29
Blunt-end darning needles	29

ALL CHILDREN CREATE

Lessons:

Level 1

LESSON 1
FIRST SELF-PORTRAIT AND PORTFOLIO

Note

This should be the first project of the year. Each student should make a folder in which to keep samples of his or her work. These folders are invaluable at parent/teacher conferences for showing students' progress.

Objectives:
- To help your students learn to include all the major body parts when drawing a person
- To demonstrate how students' skills improve over the course of a year
- To provide each student with a folder in which to keep his or her work

Materials:
- Manila folders labeled on the tabs with each student's name
- Pencils
- Crayons

Discussion:
- Tell your students that they will make folders for their papers which will be kept in the classroom until the last day of school when they may be taken home. Tell your students that they will draw pictures of themselves on the folders. Have your students name the body parts they must remember to include and call their attention to their necks, ears, eyebrows, eyelashes, noses, and all their fingers. Stress that they need to think as they draw so they won't forget anything.

Procedure:
- Direct each of your students to:

   Draw a self-portrait on the front cover of the folder using a pencil. This should be done as independently as possible with minimum help from you.

   Color the drawing so it looks like the student looks that day. You may help by asking questions such as: ''What color are your pants? Does your shirt have buttons? How long is your hair?''

- Save the folders until the end of the year when your students will draw themselves on the back covers. They will be amazed at the differences in their drawings.

- Have your students take their portfolios home at the end of the year.

LESSON 2
INTRODUCTION TO COLOR

Objectives:
- To learn that red, yellow, and blue are the primary colors and that when they are mixed with each other, all the other colors come from them
- To discover that red and yellow make orange; blue and yellow make green; and red and blue make purple

Materials:
- Eight glass containers (Jr. size baby food jars)
- Water
- Brushes
- Liquid tempera paint - red, yellow, blue
- Food coloring - red, yellow, blue
- White frosting (premixed)
- Graham crackers
- Popsicle sticks
- Small paper cups
- Paper plates
- Margaret Wise Brown, THE COLOR KITTENS, (New York: Golden Press, 1967)

Discussion:
- The discussion is carried on simultaneously with your demonstration.

Have four glass containers ¾ filled with water.

Pour some red tempera paint into one of these.

Ask your students what they think of when they see red. They will usually mention an idea like danger or anger, or an object like a fire-engine or an apple.

Do the same with blue and yellow.

Explain that red, yellow, and blue are the primary colors and that all colors, except black and white, are made from them.

Ask your students what two colors they could mix to make orange.

Pour ⅓ of the yellow paint into an empty container.

Slowly add an equal amount of the red paint so that your students can see the color change take place. (Adding a dark color to a light color shows the color change clearly.) Swirl the water with a brush to get the paint to mix well.

Clean the brush immediately in the remaining container of clear water. Tell your students that each time you mix colors you need a clean brush.

Follow the same procedure for green (adding blue to the yellow) and for purple (adding blue to the red).

Some students may want to know what will happen if all of the colors are mixed together. Use the last jar to demonstrate that you will get brown.

LESSON 2

Procedure: • Direct each of your students to:

Join two others to make a group of three. Each group will need one paper plate, three popsicle sticks, and three small paper cups half full of frosting. Warn your students not to eat their frosting yet.

Stir the frosting. You move from group to group adding food coloring to cups so each group has one cup of each color. Each student is in charge of one cup of frosting.

Experiment with mixing the colored frosting to get orange, green, and purple.

Use the popsicle sticks to mix the different colors on the paper plates.

• Distribute milk and graham crackers and let your students frost them with the colors they've mixed.

• While your students are eating, read aloud.

Illustration: • Margaret Wise Brown, THE COLOR KITTENS, (New York: Golden Press, 1967)

This book describes color mixing in story form.

LESSON 3
FINGER PAINTING — COLOR MIXING

Objective:
- To discover that mixing the primary colors (red, yellow, and blue) will make the secondary colors (orange, green, and purple)

Materials:
- Fingerpainting paper
- Fingerpaint — red, yellow, and blue
- Paint smocks
- Three tablespoons
- Newspaper
- Plastic dishpan
- Water
- Sponge for cleanup

Discussion:
- Review with your students how they mixed colors using frosting. Have them tell how to make orange, green, and purple. Write the combinations on the blackboard:
red + blue = purple; yellow + blue = green; red + yellow = orange.

Procedure:
- Demonstrate the entire procedure before having your students work independently.

   Wet the fingerpainting paper and lay it flat on the desk.

   Spoon a blob of fingerpaint on to the paper.

   Spread the paint to cover the entire paper.

   Make the design with your fingers or your whole hand.

   Show your students that the design can be erased by smoothing your hand lightly over the paper.

   Stress not using fingernails as the paper will tear.

- Bring water to your students in a plastic dishpan. (Having desks grouped makes this step easier.) The fingerpainting paper is dipped in, the excess water allowed to drip off, and the paper then smoothed on to the desk.

- Have a 'helper' spoon two colors of fingerpaint on to the wet paper. The students should choose their own colors and then guess what new color they will make.

- Allow your students to fingerpaint until a pleasing final picture is achieved. Have them print their names on the papers using their fingers.

- Hang or lay the pictures on newspaper to dry.

Caution:
- *This is a very messy project. Each student should wear a paint smock.*

sun

face

balloon

roof

hanger

mountains

wagon

book

candle

house

present

truck

Easter egg

ears

flower

LESSON 4
SHAPE COLLAGE

Objectives:
- To classify objects by shape
- To teach students how to cut shapes

Materials:
- White drawing paper. Each sheet should have one predrawn shape centered on the page. (This is for your use.)
- Black magic marker (for your use)
- Construction paper
- Scissors
- Glue
- Pencils

Discussion:
- Have your students name and describe the shapes they know. A *square* has four sides all the same; a *rectangle* has two long sides and two short sides; a *circle* is a round shape; a *triangle* has three sides; an *oval* is an egg shape.

  Hold up one of the predrawn shapes and ask, "What can you think of that is shaped like this circle?" As a suggestion is made, add details with the marker to make that object. Another paper with the same shape should then be held up and your students urged to think of something else that a circle could be. The purpose of this exercise is to get your students to realize that there are many objects that are one shape. This procedure should be followed with all five shapes, using at least four predrawn examples of each one.

Part One

Procedure:
- Demonstrate the entire procedure before having your students work independently.

  Draw a square, triangle, and rectangle.

  Cut out the shapes.

  Show how a circle can be easily made by rounding off the corners of a square. This results in a more accurate circle than drawing one.

  Ask your students if rounding off the corners of a rectangle will also make a circle. Cut, so the students discover that an oval results.

- Have your students cut a square, rectangle, circle, triangle and oval.

LESSON 4

Part Two

- Direct each of your students to:

  Cut at least one of each of the five shapes practiced in part one. They may use a different color for each shape. They may make the same shape both big and small.

  Arrange the shapes on a piece of construction paper until they are pleased with the pattern.

  Glue the shapes to the background paper.

Illustrations:

- Dr. Seuss, THE SHAPE OF ME AND OTHER STUFF, (New York: Beginner Books, 1973)

  This book shows the shapes of familiar objects through the use of silhouettes.

  Ed Emberly, THE WING ON A FLEA, (Boston: Little, Brown, & Co., 1961)

  This book shows the triangle, rectangle, and circle in many different situations.

Caution:

- *This is a long lesson. Part one and part two may be done on separate days.*

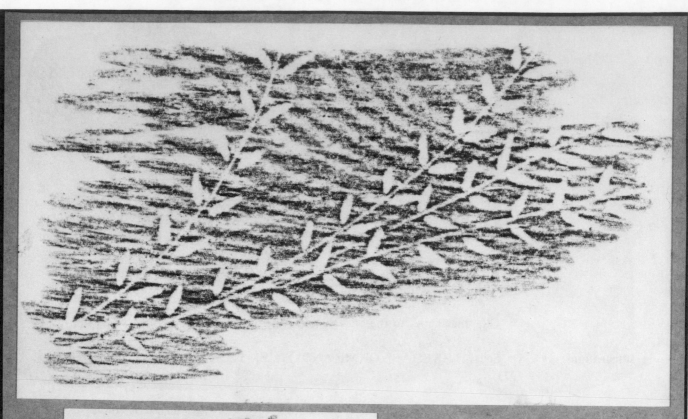

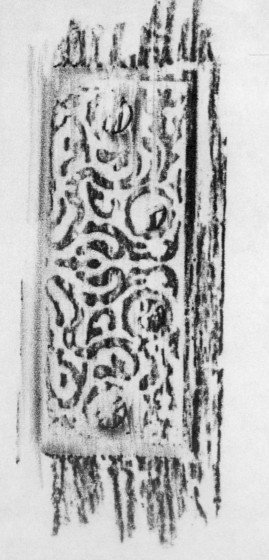

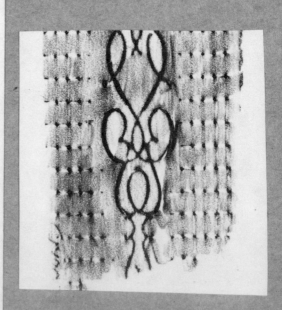

LESSON 5
TEXTURE RUBBING

Objectives:
- To help your students 'see' by using their fingers
- To make your students aware of the variety of textures occurring in man-made and natural objects

Materials:
- Examples of different textures: bark, cotton, metal, bricks, pine cones, or velvet
- Newsprint
- Black crayons

Discussion:
- The discussion should center around using your hands to help tell more about an object. Examples of different textures may be passed for your students to feel. Descriptive words such as rough, smooth, soft, and bumpy should be used. Explain to your students that these words tell about the object's texture (the actual feel of a surface).

Procedure:
- Demonstrate the entire procedure before having your students work independently.

> Cover a coin with newsprint.
>
> Hold the paper firmly.
>
> Rub a black crayon over the paper, and the image of the coin will appear.
>
> Tell your students this design is called a texture rubbing or a frottage.

- Take your students on a walk to collect texture rubbings. Some particularly interesting rubbings can be made from stop signs, manhole covers, steps on playground slides, license plates, and cornerstones.

- You may want to do the rubbings yourself. If, however, the group seems capable, your students may take turns. Each example should be labeled on the back so you can remember where they were made.

- Upon returning to the classroom, the rubbings should be looked at and discussed. If another adult is available to supervise, it works well to have two separate groups. This way, upon returning to school, each group can try to guess what the other group's rubbings are from.

- Encourage your students to make more texture rubbings at home. As they are usually very enthusiastic to try many, warn the parents with a note that it would be helpful if they labeled each rubbing. (This eliminates confusion at show and tell time when you may have to try to guess what 33 rubbings are that all look the same!)

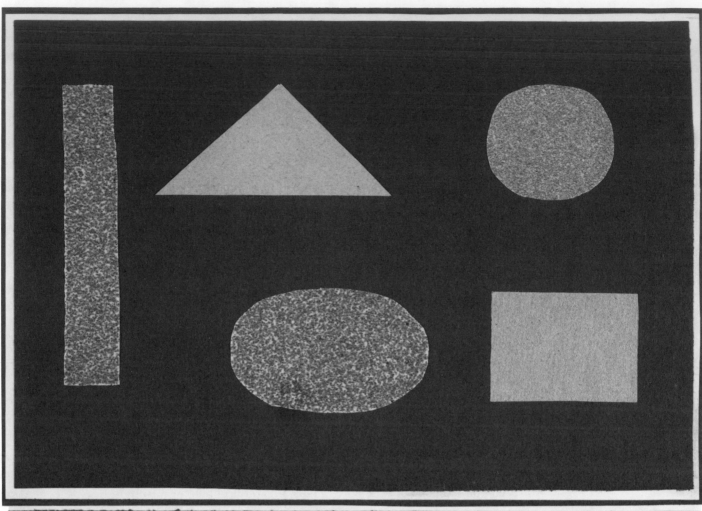

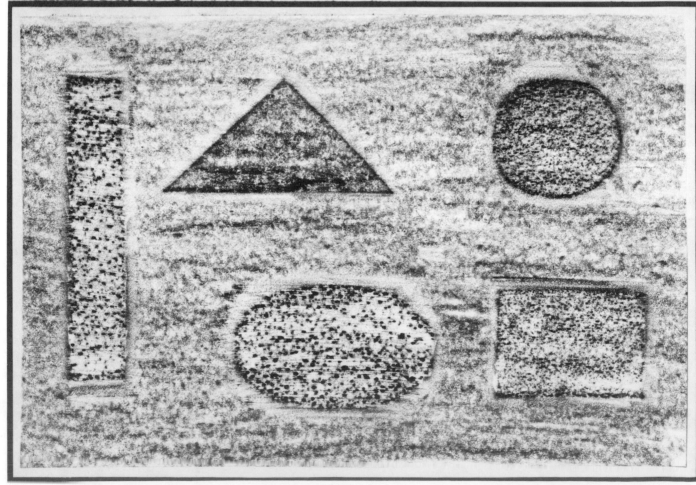

LESSON 6
TEXTURED SHAPE RUBBING

Objective: • To review the techniques of cutting shapes and making texture rubbings

Materials:
- Construction paper, 9" x 12"
- Light tagboard
- Sandpaper — different grades
- Scissors
- Glue
- Newsprint
- Crayons

Discussion: • Review with your students the techniques for cutting shapes. Stress that *circles* are made by rounding off the corners of a square; *ovals,* by rounding off the corners of a rectangle.

Review the procedure for making a texture rubbing. Stress holding the paper firmly.

Procedure: • Direct each of your students to:

Choose a combination of sandpaper and tagboard.

Cut a variety of shapes from these materials.

Arrange the shapes on the construction paper in a pleasing pattern. The sandpaper should have the rough side showing.

Glue the shapes to the construction paper.

Allow a few minutes for the glue to dry.

Place newsprint over the shape collage and make a texture rubbing.

Suggestion: • The original designs can be displayed on the bulletin board. Having your students try to match the texture rubbings to the original designs would be a good visual discrimination exercise.

LESSON 7
HALLOWEEN GOBLIN PICTURE

Objective:
- To use the imagination

Materials:
- White drawing paper, 9″ x 12″
- Crayons
- Book: "Little Orphant Annie", James Whitcomb Riley, in May Hill Arbuthnot, TIME FOR POETRY, (Chicago: Scott, Foresman & Co., 1952) p.131.

Discussion:
- Read James Whitcomb Riley's poem, *Little Orphant Annie*. Ask your students what they think a goblin is, and what it looks like. As there is no 'right' answer, this is to stimulate the imagination. You may enhance their mental image of a goblin by asking about details such as hair, teeth, eyes, hands, and skin color.

Procedure:
- Direct each of your students to:

  Draw and color a goblin.

  Add Halloween details to make a complete picture.

Suggestion:
- You may want to have extra materials available such as fur, cotton, tin foil, yarn, or packing excelsior to add interest.

LESSON 8
HALLOWEEN GHOST FAMILY

Objective: • To stimulate the imagination

Materials:
- Black construction paper, 12″ x 18″
- White construction paper, 9″ x 12″
- Varied colors of construction paper, small pieces
- Crayons
- Scissors
- Glue

Discussion: • Talk about families. Tell your students to think about their families as you ask the following questions:

> How many people are in your family?
>
> Who is the tallest?
>
> Who is the shortest?
>
> Who is the fattest?
>
> Who is the thinnest?
>
> Who wear glasses?
>
> Who has freckles?

Have your students imagine how their families would look as ghosts.

Procedure: • Demonstrate the entire procedure before having your students work independently.

Cut ghosts from the white paper, using your family as an example.

Glue the ghosts to the black paper.

Add facial features using construction paper and/or crayons.

Complete your picture by adding Halloween details such as pumpkins, bats, a full moon, or a black cat.

- Have your students each make a picture of their own family.

LESSON 9
PUMPKIN PRINTING

Note

Send a note home requesting that jack-o'-lantern lids be sent to school the day after Halloween.

Objective:
- To discover what printing is

Materials:
- Tempera paint
- Brushes
- Newsprint
- Jack-o'-lantern lids

Discussion:
- Explain the difference between printing and painting. (Printing you press and lift; painting you brush with strokes.)

    Pumpkin lids will be held by the stem. Have your students observe the bottom of the lid and discuss which parts will print. Ask, "Why won't all of it print?"

Procedure:
- Direct each of your students to:

    Paint the underside of the pumpkin lid with tempera.

    Press the lid on to the newsprint and lift it off carefully to make a print.

- Two or three prints can be made from one painting.

Suggestion:
- All of your students may not have a pumpkin top. They can share.

Caution:
- *This is a very short, purely exploratory project.*

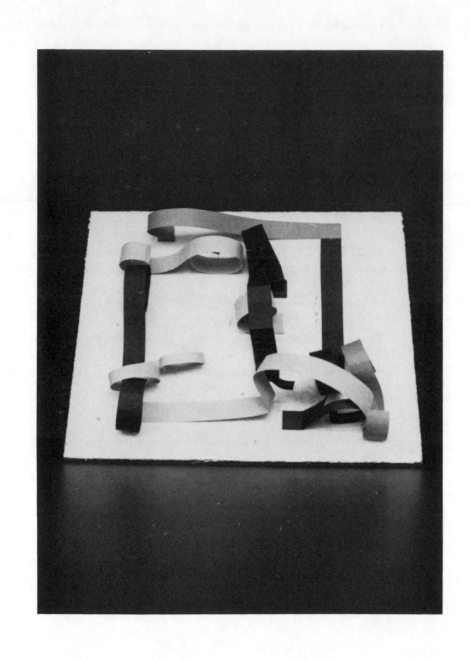

LESSON 10
PAPER STRIP SCULPTURES

Objectives:
- To learn what a sculpture is
- To create a paper sculpture

Materials:
- Construction paper in various dark colors, 12″ x 18″
- Yellow or white paper strips, 1″ x 12″
- Glue

Discussion:
- Define sculpture (a form that can be seen from all sides; it is not flat like a picture). Tell your students that statues are one kind of sculpture; that is, forms of people. You might bring a figurine to class as an example.

  Tell your students that sculptures can be of things or ideas as well as people. They will make a paper sculpture that looks like roads and rollercoasters.

Procedure:
- Demonstrate the entire procedure before having your students work independently.

  Glue paper strips to the construction paper base so that they are not flat. Strips may be curved, intertwined, layered, or looped.

  Stress that the strips must be held in place until the glue has a chance to partially dry.

- Let your students fill their papers with varied forms.

Illustrations:
- Pictures of rollercoasters
- Pictures of multi-level highway interchanges

  These demonstrate the design in architecture that your students should appreciate with heightened awareness.

- Joanne Oppenheim, HAVE YOU SEEN ROADS, (New York: Young Scott Books, 1969)

  The pictures in this book should make your students more aware of the design found in man made structures.

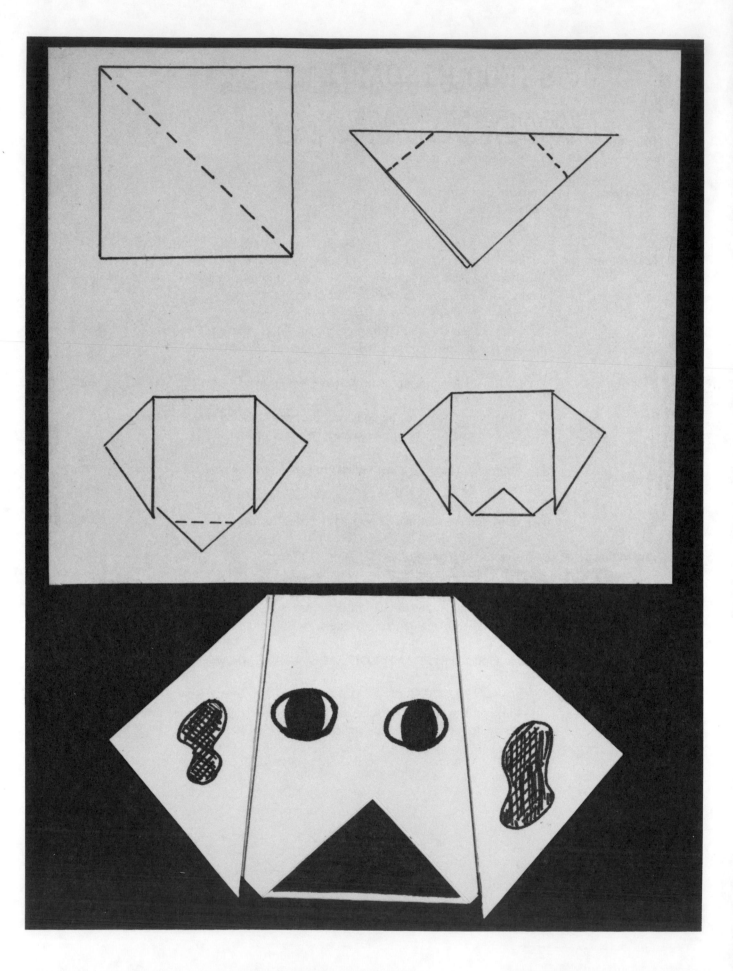

LESSON 11
ORIGAMI — PAPER FOLDING

Objectives:
- To discover the fun of making folded paper objects
- To listen carefully and follow directions
- To learn what origami is

Part One

Materials:
- Brown and white construction paper, 9″ x 9″
- Crayons

Part Two

- A single sheet of newspaper for each student

Part Three

- White drawing paper, 6″ x 6″

Discussion:
- Have your students talk about all the things they can do with paper such as cut, tear, glue and fold it.

  Discuss the Japanese traditional art form, *origami*, which involves only paper folding. Japanese children learn to fold paper into forms before they start school. Discuss how origami can be both decorative and functional.

Part One

Procedure:
- Direct each of your students to:

  Choose a piece of brown or white construction paper.

  Fold the paper diagonally, matching corners.

  Lay the paper with the folded edge at the top.

  Take the upper right hand corner and fold it so it is pointed straight down.

  Do the same with the upper left hand corner. These make the dog's ears.

  Fold the bottom point up to make the dog's nose. Be sure to fold both layers together.

  Add details with crayon: eyes, nose, and spots. Mention that the students are not to make a mouth.

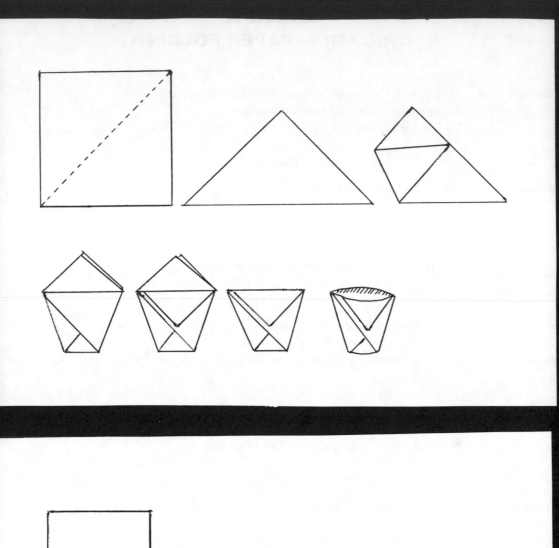

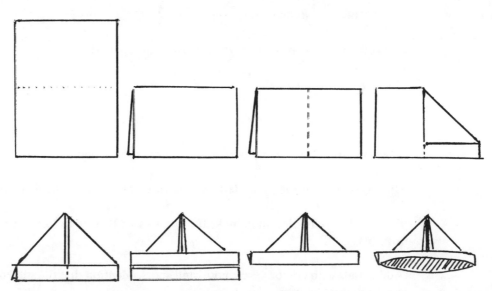

LESSON 11

Part Two

Procedure: • Direct each of your students to:

Fold a single sheet of newspaper in half, matching corners.

Fold the paper in half the other way and open. The fold marks the center of the paper.

Fold the upper left hand corner down to the center fold.

Do the same with the upper right hand corner.

Fold the top strip up and the bottom strip back. The bottom of the paper is double.

Open the hat and wear it.

Suggestion: • You may want to have your students secure the ends of the hat with glue to make it more durable.

Part Three

Procedure: • Direct each of your students to:

Fold their white drawing paper in half diagonally, matching corners.

Lay the paper with the folded edge nearest them.

Take the lower right hand corner of the triangle and fold it so it touches the left hand edge of the triangle.

Take the lower left hand corner of the triangle and fold it so it touches the right hand side of the triangle.

Fold the top layer forward and the bottom layer backward. The top of the paper is double.

Open the cup.

• You may have your students use their cups for a milk break.

Caution: • *The directions may be difficult for some students to follow, but with supervision, all will be able to end up with a cup. The pride of accomplishment justifies the possible frustrations.*

LESSON 12
TOTEM POLES — SCULPTURE

Objectives:
- To learn about a Native American art form
- To create a three-dimensional sculpture

Materials:
- Pictures and/or examples of Native American art and designs
- Miscellaneous boxes with covers: oatmeal, salt, shoe, cereal, etc. (1 per student)
- Tempera paint
- Brushes
- Scissors
- Glue
- Construction paper scraps in a variety of colors
- Newspapers

Discussion:
- Ask your students if they know what a totem pole is. Totem poles were made by the Indians of the Northwest. Totem poles have a combination of fish, bird, and human forms. No two poles are the same. Some are 70' high; some are only a few feet high. All are brightly painted. Some totem poles were attached to the front of the house; some stood in front of the house; some were inside the house to support the roof; and some were burial columns that held the body or ashes of the dead. Totemism is the belief in the animal ancestors of a clan and each pole shows the simplified animal motifs that belong to that family. Tell the students that totem poles are sculptures (forms that can be seen from all sides; they are not flat like a picture). Talk about Indian design, especially examples that show stylized faces. Tell your students they are each going to make one part of a totem pole.

Procedure:
- Direct each of your students to:

    Glue or secure with masking tape the loose box cover.

    Cover the desk with newspaper.

    Paint the box on all sides as the sculptures will be seen from all sides.

    Set the box aside to dry.

    Cut facial features from the construction paper scraps. Stress remembering eyes, nose, mouth, and ears. Features can lay flat on the box or extend out.

    Glue the face on to the box.

- Arrange the boxes into several totem poles and glue them together.

- Display the totem poles in the room or hallway.

Illustration:
- Shirley Glubok, THE ART OF THE SOUTHWEST INDIANS, (New York: The Macmillan Co., 1971)

    This book will help extend your students' appreciation of Native American art and design.

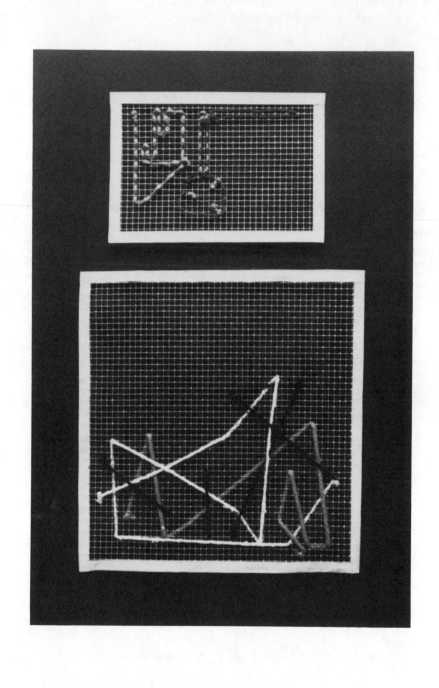

LESSON 13
HARDWARE CLOTH STITCHERY

Objectives:
- To introduce your students to stitchery
- To develop eye/hand coordination

Materials:
- Quarter-inch mesh hardware cloth, 6" x 9", precut with tin snips
- Masking tape (taped around the edges of the hardware cloth)
- Rug yarn

Discussion:
- Talk about sewing. Ask your students if they know what a stitchery is (making a picture or design by sewing). Tell your students they are going to be sewing and making a stitchery with yarn but they will not use a needle.

Procedure:
- Demonstrate the entire procedure before having your students work independently.

    Tie the end of the yarn to one of the meshes with a double knot before beginning to stitch.

    Poke the yarn through the holes to create a design or a picture. The yarn can go through every mesh, like weaving, or it can skip meshes in any direction. Yarn lines can cross.

    Twist the yarn between two fingers to make a point if the yarn begins to ravel.

    Tie the end of the yarn to a mesh in a double knot before beginning with a new color.

- Allow your students to stitch a design or a picture and use whatever colors they wish.

Illustration:
- A stamped needlepoint canvas with a design partly worked. This will illustrate to your students the adult counterpart of this activity.

Suggestion:
- You may want to have parent volunteers present for this project as your students may need help getting started.

LESSON 14
CRAYON RESIST GIFT WRAP

Objectives:
- To create a gift wrap
- To learn how to work with water colors
- To explore the technique of crayon resist

Materials:
- Color crayons
- Water color paint boxes
- Water containers
- Newsprint or white paper large enough to wrap gift
- Paper towels

Discussion:
- Ask your students to name things they think of during the holiday season. Make a quick outline drawing on the blackboard of each suggestion. Try to get at least twelve ideas.

Introduce your students to the use and care of watercolors:

Dip your brush in water.

Lay your brush on the watercolor square sideways, the back of the brush slightly raised.

Roll the brush over the square so all sides get covered with color.

Do not put the point of your brush straight down into the paint. This will cause the bristles to spread and will soon ruin the brush.

Every time you use a new color, rinse your brush.

Always leave your paintbox clean. If there is any water left in the paint, roll your clean brush over the square to get rid of it.

Leave your brush clean and pointed.

Part One

Procedure:
- Direct each of your students to:

Fold newsprint in half several times to make rectangles approximately 3" x 4".

Unfold the paper.

Color a different symbol of the holidays with crayons in each rectangle.

Part Two

- Direct each of your students to:

Paint over each drawing with watercolors using a different color in each rectangle. The crayon drawing will resist the watercolor and be enclosed by the color.

Leave a small margin of white between each rectangle. This will keep the colors from running together.

Suggestion:
- If you are making the decoupage boards, it works well to do part one of the gift wrap simultaneously with staining the boards. The students can be called three at a time to work with you on staining.

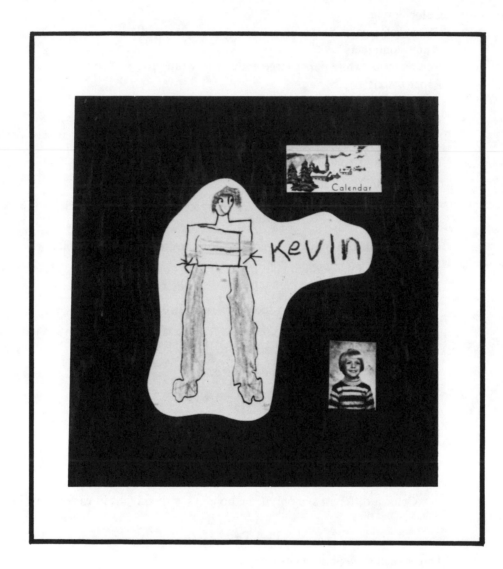

LESSON 15
SELF-PORTRAIT — HOLIDAY GIFT — DECOUPAGE

Note

At the beginning of December send a note to parents requesting a photograph of their child, sandpaper, and a board about 10" x 12" suitable for sanding (not paneling.) Tell them these are for a present. If they have extra scrap lumber they may send more than one board.

Objectives:
- To draw a self-portrait
- To make a gift

Materials:
- Manila paper
- Crayons
- Scissors
- Newspapers
- *Watersoluable* wood stain
- Sandpaper
- Mod Podge
- Old paint brushes (about 2" wide)
- Optional:
  - Small calendars
  - Photos of students (about 1" x 3")
  - Disposable plastic gloves (from school cafeteria)

Discussion:
- Tell the students they will be making a present for their parents and they should try to do their very best. Review the parts of the body by playing a quick game of ''Simon Says.'' Tell your students that a portrait is a painting of a real person and they are going to make a self-portrait.

Part One

Procedure:
- Direct each of your students to:
  Draw a self-portrait. Stress remembering all body parts. You may want to do a drawing on the blackboard to help them.
  Color the picture showing how they look that day. Stress details such as hair, eye color, length of hair, and clothing colors. This is just a practice drawing. Your students will make their final drawing later in the day or on the following day.

Part Two

- Direct each of your students to:
  Draw and color their final self-portrait. Stress making the picture complete, but let them work independently.
  Check their picture to see if they have forgotten anything.
  Print their name close to the picture using a dark crayon.
- You cut a blob-like shape around the drawing and the name.

Suggestion:
- At the end of part two, advise your students to wear old clothes on the next day as they will be working with wood stain.

LESSON 15

Part Three

Procedure: • Direct each of your students to:

Print their name on the back of their board.

Open sheets of newspaper and place the board on it.

Sand the front and edges of the boards. Stress following the wood grain. (This sanding will be far from perfect. It is more to teach the students the process than to smooth the wood.)

Wipe the board and carefully fold up the newspapers and throw them away. Stress not getting sawdust all over.

Part Four

Procedure: • Direct each of your students to:

Work in a group of three under your supervision at a newspaper covered table.

Wear one plastic glove while staining, holding their other hand *behind* their back.

Wipe stain on their board with a rag. Your students should stain the top side and you do the edges to speed up the process.

Set the board aside to dry until the next day.

• Cleanup is simplified if there is another adult present to help the students remove gloves and wash their hands.

• The rest of the class can be independently working on the crayon resist gift wrap.

Part Five

Procedure: • Direct each of your students to:

Sit in a group of four.

Place a half sheet of newspaper under their board.

Keep track of their own photograph and drawing which should have been distributed to them.

Paint one coat of Mod Podge on their board. You should move from group to group with a pie plate full of Mod Podge and four brushes. Your students should be expected to do some individual seat work while they wait their turn to decoupage. This part of the project takes a long time and they will need to be occupied.

Wait until the Mod Podge becomes dry and clear.

Paint a second coat. You should immediately position the drawing and photo of each student on the wet board and smooth out the air bubbles.

Wait until the board dries clear again.

Paint the third coat of Mod Podge directly over the drawing and photo. This seals them permanently on the board.

Set aside to dry until the next day.

• Glue the calendars on the boards for your students.

LESSON 16
PAPER SNOWFLAKES

Objectives:
- To learn how to cut a symmetrical pattern
- To learn that all snowflakes are unique

Materials:
- Mimeograph paper, 9″ x 9″
- Scissors

Discussion:
- Your discussion could come after a trip outside to observe snowflakes as they land on mittens and hands. Tell your students that no two snowflakes are ever exactly alike and that if they were to look at snowflakes under a microscope, they could see this. Explain that instead of using a microscope they will make snowflakes and see that they all turn out differently.

Procedure:
- Direct each of your students to:

  Fold the paper in half, and then in half again the other way. The result is a square 4½″ x 4½″.

  Fold the square in half diagonally to make a triangle.

  Cut blob like shapes from the triangle. Be sure that each cut begins and ends on the same side; do not cut through to another edge.

  Open the paper to see the resulting snowflake.

- Have your students make at least one more snowflake on their own. This way they will discover that each snowflake is indeed different.

- Display one snowflake from each student to illustrate the fact that all snowflakes are unique.

LESSON 17
PAPER WEAVING

Objective: • To learn the over/under concept of weaving

Materials: • Construction paper, 12″ x 18″, precut to form loom

(Fold the paper in half lengthwise. Beginning on the fold make six cuts, stopping 2″ from the top and spaced so there are seven even strips.) Each student needs one loom.

• Construction paper strips, 2″ x 12″, all colors
Each student needs six.

Discussion: • Ask your students if they know what weaving is and how it is done. A piece of burlap shows the over/under weave clearly.

Procedure: • Demonstrate the entire procedure before having your students work independently.

Start weaving at the top of the loom.

Weave one strip *over* the first loom strip, *under* the second, *over* the third . . .

Weave the second strip *under* the first loom strip, *over* the second, then *under* . . .

Repeat the above steps.

• Have your students fill their looms with their varied colored strips.

LESSON 18
TORN PAPER SNOWMAN COLLAGE

Objectives:
- To discover that torn paper gives a soft edge
- To develop eye/hand coordination

Materials
- Blue construction paper, 12″ x 18″
- White construction paper, 9″ x 12″
- Miscellaneous colored construction paper
- White chalk
- Scissors
- Glue

Discussion:
- Compare winter to the other three seasons. List activities that occur only in winter. Focus on building snowmen. Talk about the three sizes of snowballs you need for a snowman. Ask the students if the balls are *truly* round. If not, why not?

  Tell your students they are to make a winter picture.
  The only requirement is that it must include at least one snowman.

Procedure:
- Demonstrate the entire procedure before having your students work independently.

  Tear the circles for a snowman. Tell your students torn edges will look soft like real snowballs.

  Cut everything else. Talk about what a snowman could wear.

  Stress making a complete winter picture. White chalk can be used for details.

- Tell your students to have everything cut, torn, and arranged on their large blue paper before they glue. This allows them to move pieces if they want to rearrange any.

Illustration:
- Ezra Jack Keats, THE SNOWY DAY, (New York: Scholastic Book Service, 1971)

  The illustrations in this book are paper collages.

LESSON 19
LIFE-SIZE PEOPLE DRAWINGS

Objectives:
- To learn to include major body parts in a drawing
- To improve cutting skills

Materials:
- White wrapping paper
- Scissors
- Tempera paint
- Brushes
- Pencils or pens
- Black markers

Discussion:
- Have your students name the parts of the body. You may want to write them on the blackboard. Play a quick game of "Simon Says" having your students touch the body parts as they are named. Tell your students they will make a life-sized drawing of themselves.

Procedure:
- Direct each of your students to:

  Work with a partner. (One will trace the body outline while the other lays on a piece of wrapping paper.)

  Lay on a piece of wrapping paper with all fingers spread, arms away from the body, and legs apart.

  Trace the body outline with pencil or ball point pen.

  Paint their outline to show how they look that day, being careful to include such details as eye and hair color, clothing patterns, buttons and collars.

  Print their name on their picture with a black marker after the paint has dried.

  Cut out the picture, being particularly careful as they cut around the fingers.

Suggestion:
- It would be helpful to get several upper level students to assist your students with the tracing.

- These make a nice wall display for the room or hall.

Caution:
- *You may want to have the students work in small groups on separate days because of the size of the pictures.*

LESSON 20
VALENTINE STITCHERY

Objective:
- To create a stitchery

Materials:
- Styrofoam meat trays, 8″ x 10″
- Blunt pointed darning needles (stuck through a piece of construction paper so needle will not roll and get lost)
- Yarn (mostly red)
- Newsprint
- Crayons
- Scotch tape

Discussion:
- Demonstrate and talk about the running stitch. It goes in and out, in and out, in a line. Show your students the satin stitch where stitches are close together and side by side. Tell them it is used for filling in solid shapes.

Procedure:
- Demonstrate the entire procedure before having your students work independently.

    Cut several hearts of varied size from the newsprint.

    Lay the hearts on the *back* of the meat tray.

    Arrange them in a pleasing pattern.

    Trace around the hearts lightly with crayon.

    Poke holes along the crayon lines with your needle approximately ¼ to ½ inch apart.

    Thread the needle with yarn 18″ long.

    Starting from the back, poke the needle through the hole and pull yarn through leaving a short tail.

    Secure the tail to the back of the tray with Scotch tape.

    Follow the holes using the running stitch.

    End on the back and secure the yarn end with tape.

- Your students may want to stitch a border and make some areas solid.

Caution:
- *Stress care in working with needles when sitting close together. Do not extend your arm while holding needle as you do not want to hit anyone with it, particularly not anyone's eye.*

- *Have your students check each stitch as they make it to see that the yarn is pulled all the way through.*

- *Your students should know how to cut hearts before starting this project.*

LESSON 21
STYROFOAM AND TOOTHPICK SCULPTURE

Objectives:
- To learn what a sculpture is
- To create an abstract sculpture

Materials:
- Styrofoam meat trays or blocks of styrofoam to act as a base for the sculpture
- Styrofoam packing materials in various shapes: i.e., peanuts, discs, curls
- Round toothpicks

Discussion:
- Define sculpture (a form that can be seen from all sides; it is not flat like a picture.) Tell your students that statues are one kind of sculpture; that is, forms of people. You might bring a figurine to class as an example. Tell your students they will make a different kind of sculpture — an abstract sculpture (something that is not real), and perhaps their imaginations will help them see forms in it.

Procedure:
- Demonstrate the entire procedure before having your students work independently.

  Use a styrofoam block or an upside down meat tray as the base.

  Construct the sculpture by connecting styrofoam discs, peanuts, and curls to the base and to each other with toothpicks.

- Let your students construct their sculptures as high and as complex as desired.

Caution:
- *These sculptures are extremely fragile.*

LESSON 22
SCRIBBLE DESIGN

Objectives:
- To discover the fun of making an abstract line design
- To see how mounting enhances a picture

Materials:
- Manila paper, 9" x 12"
- Construction paper, 9" x 12", in a variety of bright colors
- Crayons
- Scissors
- Glue

Discussion:
- Tell your students that usually they need to be neat and careful when they color. Today they may also scribble.

Procedure:
- Demonstrate the entire procedure before having your students work independently.

    Draw a scribble with black crayon. The scribble should have large open areas and not touch the edge of the paper.

    Color each section of the scribble heavily using a variety of colors. Adjoining sections should be filled in with different colors.

    Cut the scribble out along the outside edge after it is colored.

    Position it on the colored construction paper.

    Glue.

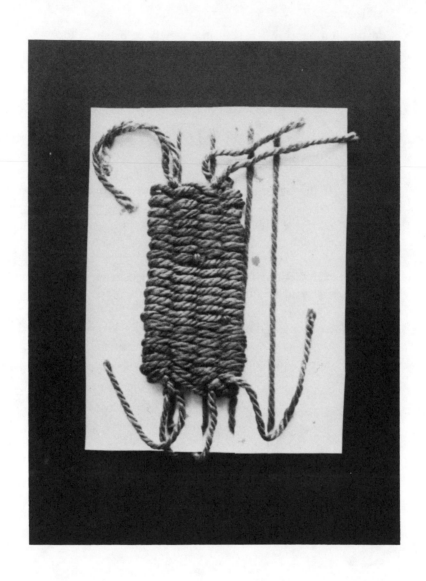

LESSON 23
WOVEN BRACELET

Objectives:
- To further your students' knowledge of weaving
- To learn the words *warp* and *weft*

Materials:
- Cardboard loom which you have prepared
    One side of a ½ gallon milk carton works well for this.
    Cut four slits about ¾" long and about ½" from each other on each end — directly opposite each other.
- Yarn, 56" long
    36" long (Students love varigated yarn if available)
- Masking tape

Discussion:
- Review the over/under concept of weaving
    Define *warp* (the lengthwise thread that is strung on the loom, and *weft* (threads that are woven over and under the warp.)

Procedure:
- Demonstrate the entire procedure before having your students work independently.

    Fasten the 56" long piece of yarn in the center of the back of the loom with a small piece of masking tape. The back is the side with printing. The front is plain so nothing will distract your students from weaving.

    Pull the yarn through the end slot to the front.

    Wrap the yarn around the loom lengthwise, catching it in each slot in order. You should have four straight lengths of yarn pulled firmly across the front of the loom.

    Fasten the warp end on the back with a second piece of masking tape. Your loom is dressed (ready for weaving.)

    Use a 36" long piece of yarn for the weft.

    Knot the weft to the first warp string near the top of the loom.

    Weave over, under, over, under — and you are at the end of the warp. Because the last move was under, when you start back it must be over. Each time you start with over, then under, over, under.

    Do not pull the weft yarn too tightly or the edges will pull in.

    Push the yarn up as you finish each row to have it meet the row above.

    Knot the weft thread on the warp when the loom is full.

    Cut the warp at the center back and remove the weaving from the loom.

    Tie the first and second warp threads together in a double knot close to the weaving and tie the third and fourth warp threads together at both ends. This keeps the weaving from unravelling.

- Your students can wear these as bracelets by tying them on their wrists.

Caution:
- *This is a long and complicated project and your students will need a lot of supervision, but this is a project they thoroughly enjoy.*

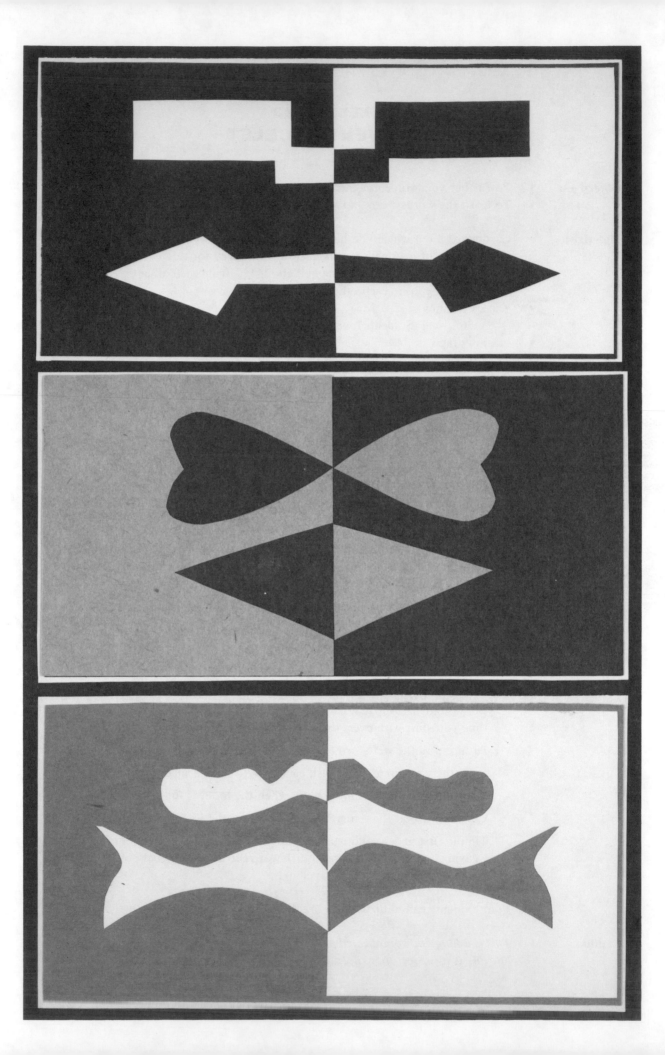

LESSON 24
POSITIVE–NEGATIVE (OPPOSITES)

Objectives:
- To develop pasting and cutting skills
- To be aware of how things look different (and yet similar) when reversed

Materials:
- Dark construction paper, 12" x 18"
- Light construction paper, 9" x 12"
- Scissors
- Glue

Discussion:
- The discussion should center around the concept of opposites. Ask your students to name some opposites. If they are unfamiliar with the term you may prompt them. For example: If you are not happy, you are _____.

  Explain that they will make an 'opposite' picture.

Procedure:
- Demonstrate the entire procedure before having your students work independently.

  Cut two blob-like shapes from the smaller sheet. Begin and end cutting on the same 12" edge.

  Glue the small sheet on to the larger paper, matching corners, so the cut edge is in the center.

  Lay the cut out forms back in their original place, then tip them back on to the dark paper.

  Glue.

LESSON 25
CLAY ANIMALS

Objectives:
- To learn techniques for working with clay
- To create a clay sculpture

Materials:
- Modeling clay
- Table knives or popsicle sticks
- Two pieces of wrapping paper

    Use a magic marker to outline areas indicating a farm and a zoo. The students will be placing their clay animals on the paper to complete the display.

- Wax paper

Discussion:
- Have your students briefly name animals and tell whether they live in a zoo or on a farm. Tell your students they will make a clay animal. It will be a sculpture (a form that can be seen from all sides. It is not flat like a picture.).

    Demonstrate clay techniques to the students.

    Roll clay around the palms of your hand to make a sphere.

    Roll clay back and forth between your palms to make a coil or a snake.

    Pinch and squeeze the clay to make a form.

    Pound the clay flat and cut in a shape with a knife or a popsicle stick.

    Print a design in the clay by using the tip of a knife or a stick. (This is intaglio printing: a design or line carved below the surface.)

    Demonstrate how to make four-legged animals.

    Roll a cylinder of clay. Cut through each end of the clay with a popsicle stick. Bend the resulting two sections of each end down to make legs. This eliminates the problem of pinched-on legs falling off.

Procedure:
- Direct each of your students to:

    Lay wax paper on the desk for a working surface.

    Experiment with all the clay techniques before beginning the animal.

    Choose and make any animal they want.

- When the animals are completed, place them on the appropriate wrapping paper scene.

LESSON 26
WATERCOLOR KITES

Objective: • To explore the medium

Materials: • White drawing paper, 12″ x 18″
  • Scissors
  • Watercolor paint boxes
  • Yarn for kite tails
  • Miscellaneous construction paper scraps
  • Newspaper
  • Paper towels

Discussion: • This project should be done in the spring, and can be incorporated into a discussion of activities that are done in this season. Stress both the similarities and differences that exist among the seasons.

Demonstrate the use and care of watercolors:

Dip your brush in water.

Lay your brush on the watercolor square sideways, the back of the brush slightly raised.

Roll the brush over the square so all sides get covered with color.

Do not put the point of your brush straight down into the paint square. This will cause the bristles to spread and will ruin the brush.

Every time you use a new color rinse your brush.

Leave your paintbox clean. If there is any water left in the paint squares, roll your clean brush over the square to get rid of it.

Leave your brush clean and pointed.

Procedure: • Demonstrate the entire procedure before having your students work independently.

Fold the paper in half, matching corners.

Fold the paper in half the other way.

Cut the resulting rectangle from corner to corner. Start on a corner where one edge is folded and one is open. Fold —

Open the paper to see the kite shape.

Fold

  • Let your students paint the kites as they choose.

  • While the kites are drying, your students can attach the yarn tails and tail pieces cut from construction paper scraps.

  • If they wish, your students may cut eyes, nose and mouth from construction paper and glue them on the kite when it is dry.

LESSON 27
BUTTERFLIES — SPONGE PRINTING

Objective:
- To discover what printing is

Materials:
- Tissue paper, 15" x 20", all colors
- Black or white pipe cleaners
- Sponges cut in small cubes
- Pincher clothespins to attach to sponges for handles
- Tempera paint — white
- Brushes

Discussion:
- Discuss butterflies, their colors, how they fly, and how light they must be to rest on a flower.

  Define printing (stamping or pressing an object covered with paint on to a paper; when lifted off, the object leaves a print).

Procedure:
- Direct each of your students to:

  Select a sheet of tissue paper.

  Attach a clothespin handle to a sponge.

  Use a brush to paint the sponge with tempera.

  Press the painted side of the sponge on the paper and lift it carefully off. (Stress printing as opposed to painting with the sponge.)

  Print many patterns on the tissue paper.

  Clean up the brushes and paint while the paper dries.

  Gather the paper together in the middle, twist a pipe cleaner around it, and let the two equal ends extend up for antennae.

- When all the students are done, play soft, 'butterfly' music and let them fly their butterflies gently. This can be done while they are in their seats.

Illustration:
- Pictures of butterflies

  Show your students that butterflies do come in all colors. Talk about the markings on their wings. Tell them that these are some of nature's most beautiful designs.

Dear Mr. Jones,
Thank you!

Love,
The First Grade

I liked the heart machine for "zapping" people.

The ambulance was neat.

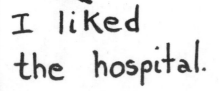

I liked the hospital.

Hearing my heart beat was fun.

LESSON 28
THANK YOU MURAL — GROUP PROJECT

Objectives:
- To allow students to say thank you in their own special way
- To learn the importance of a thank you letter
- To do a recall drawing

Materials:
- Sheet of white wrapping paper long enough for all of your students to sit side by side along the bottom edge.
- Magic markers — at least one per student. The students can share colors.

Discussion:
- This is to take place after your class has made a field trip to some point of interest in the town or even around the school. Let your students tell what they enjoyed most. Stress the point of always thanking people who have done something nice for you. Tell your students that they will make a group thank you letter in the form of a mural (a long wall decoration).

Procedure:
- Direct each of your students to:

    Listen while you read aloud a letter you have written across the top of the sheet. For example:

    Dear Chief Jones,
    Thank you for showing us the fire station. Sitting on the fire truck and blowing the siren was fun. These are the things that we liked best.
    Love,
    The first grade

    Sit side by side along the bottom edge of the stretched out wrapping paper. (The hall can be used if the room is not long enough.) Stress being careful not to tear the paper.

    Draw the thing he or she liked best.

- Label each drawing using your student's own dictated words.

- Deliver the rolled up thank you letter.

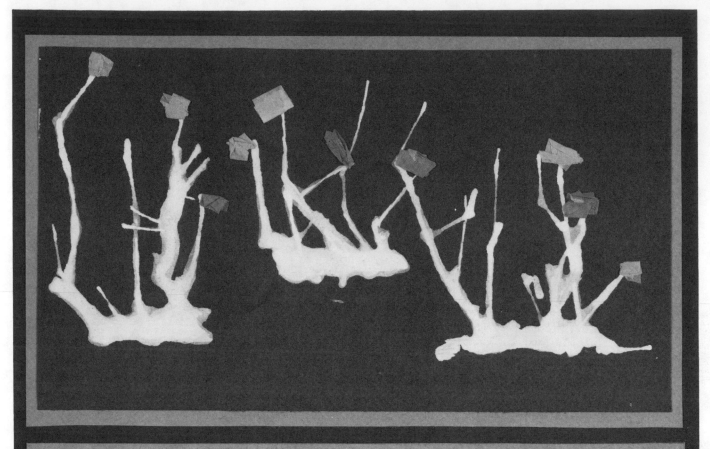

LESSON 29
SPRING FLOWERS — ACCIDENTAL DESIGN

Objectives:
- To stretch the imagination
- To experiment with controlled, accidental design

Materials:
- Construction paper, 9" x 12", in pastel colors
- Thin black tempera paint in plastic bowls
- Teaspoons
- Straws
- Tissue paper scraps — all colors
- Glue

Discussion:
- Discuss with your students the difference between accidental and planned design. An example of planned design is thinking of a subject to paint and then painting it. An example of accidental design is splashing or dropping paint on a piece of paper. Sometimes imagination helps us see a picture in an accidental design; sometimes we see only an interesting shape. Tell your students they will create a flower garden using accidental design.

Procedure:
- Demonstrate the entire procedure before having your students work independently.

  Lay a piece of construction paper so the 12" sides are horizontal.

  Use a spoon to place tempera paint on your paper. The paint should be placed in a horizontal line at least two inches up from the bottom edge.

  Blow through a straw to direct the paint upward like stems of flowers and grass.

  Let the paint dry.

  Attach torn pieces of tissue paper as flowers. Tissue should be folded or crumpled with a dot of glue in the center so it will not lie flat on the paper.

- Let your students make one or several clusters of stems on their papers.

LESSON 30
FATHER'S DAY PORTRAIT — DESIGN

Objectives:
- To make a design
- To see that design is used in clothing
- To make a recall drawing

Materials:
- White drawing paper, 9″ x 12″
- Pastel construction paper, 9″ x 12″
- Crayons
- Scissors
- Glue

Discussion:
- Have your students observe the design and pattern in their own clothing: for example, plaid, stripe, polka dot, floral print, paisley, herringbone, and hound's-tooth check. Have available several neckties; note the design in each.

  Tell your students that Father's Day comes after school is out so this is an early Father's Day present. Define a portrait (a picture of a real person).

Procedure:
- Demonstrate the entire procedure before having your students work independently.

  Draw your father's portrait on the white drawing paper. Make it large enough to fill the page and be sure it includes his neck.

  Color the portrait.

  Stress remembering how your father looks.

  Draw a necktie on the colored sheet as long as the paper. (It would be helpful to draw this shape on the board so your students will know how it should look.)

  Design a pattern for the necktie and color it.

  Cut out the necktie.

  Glue the knot of the tie on your father's portrait.

- Have each student draw their own father's portrait and create their own necktie design.

Caution:
- *Some of your students might not have a father. This could then be the portrait of an uncle, a big brother, a grandfather, or a special friend.*

ALL CHILDREN CREATE

Lessons:

Level 2

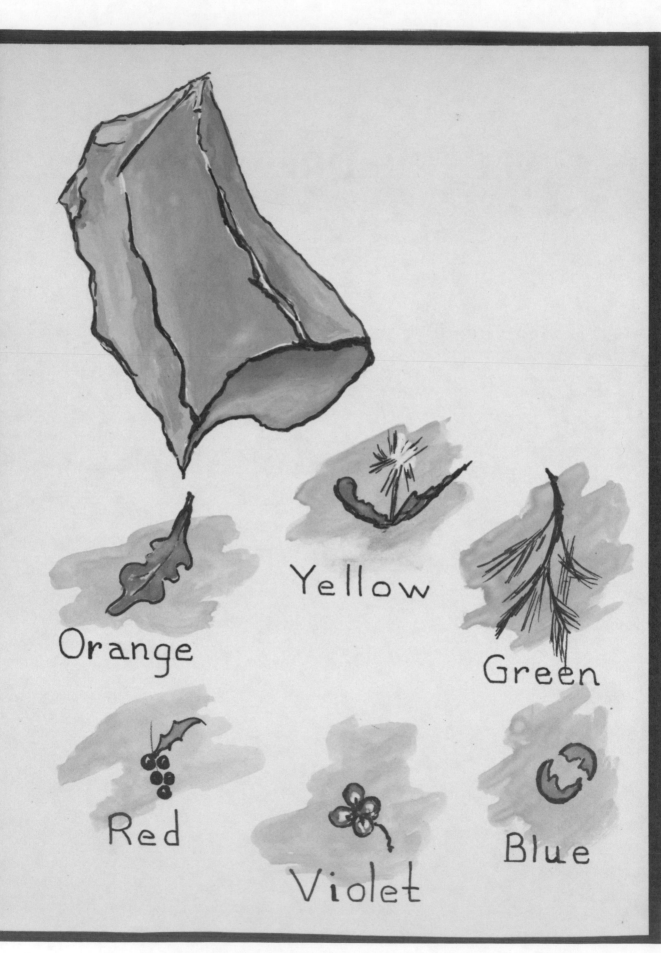

Orange

Yellow

Green

Red

Violet

Blue

LESSON 31
COLOR WALK

Objective: • To discover that colors have many shades

Materials: • Small paper bags — one per student
 • Large sheet of wrapping paper, 6' long, divided into squares that have been labeled with color names

Red	Green	Purple	Black	White
Blue	Yellow	Orange	Brown	

Use colored markers to write the appropriate color; i.e., red marker writes red

Discussion: • Have your students name the nine common colors: red, blue, green, yellow, purple, orange, black, brown, and white. Your discussion will be expanded at the end of this activity.

Procedure: • Direct each of your students to:

Carry a paper bag as you go on a "color walk."

Collect one object of each color to place in the bag.

Place the objects on the appropriate square of wrapping paper when you return to the classroom.

Sit in a circle around the paper for a discussion.

 • Your students should discover that each color has a variety of shades. For example, blue is not always the same blue.

Caution: • *Some colors are harder to find than others.*

Illustrations: • Sylvia Root Tester, A WORLD OF COLOR, (Elgin, Illinois; The Child's World, 1939)

 • John Reiss, COLORS, (Scarsdale, N. Y.: Bradbury Press, 1969)

These books show color mixing as well as illustrating the variety of objects that come in each color.

LESSON 32
PURPLE COLLAGE

Objectives:
- To discover that colors have different shades and tints
- To explore texture
- To make a single color collage

Materials:
- Book: Crockett Johnson, HAROLD AND THE PURPLE CRAYON, (New York: Harper and Row Publishers, Inc., 1955)
- Miscellaneous purple materials; e.g., material, yarn, wallpaper, construction paper, pipe cleaners, cellophane, tissue paper, buttons, rickrack, gift wrap, ribbon, paint, crayons, and chalk
- Lavender construction paper, 12" x 18"
- Scissors
- Glue

Discussion:
- Have your students name all the purple things they can think of. List them on the blackboard. Ask your students if purple always looks the same. They should be able to say that purple can be light or dark. Mention that purple also has two different names that they probably know — lavender and violet — to indicate different shades of the same color.

  Ask your students if they know what a collage is (a composition made by gluing various materials to a background).

  Show the class all the purple materials you have collected and discuss the different shades of purple and the different textures. Read the book *Harold and the Purple Crayon* aloud to the class. Tell your students they are going to make a purple day collage picture like Harold did. It can be something they might see, or do, or feel. It can be one thing in their day, a part of their day, or the whole day.

Procedure:
- Direct each of your students to:

  Decide on a picture or a theme for the collage. For those who seem hesitant, you might suggest a few ideas.

  Select the materials to be used in the collage.

  Arrange the collage on the lavender construction paper.

  Glue.

LESSON 33
FINGERPAINT PRINT

Objectives:
- To create a monoprint
- To review color mixing; that is, red + blue = purple; red + yellow = orange; blue + yellow = green; red + blue + yellow = brown

Materials:
- Fingerpaint - red, yellow, and blue
- Newsprint
- Paint smocks
- Water
- Paper towels
- Sponge and cleanser for cleanup

Discussion:
- Review with your students the colors needed to make green, orange, purple, and brown. Write the combinations on the blackboard. Tell your students they are going to fingerpaint and then lift a print from their paintings. Ask them how they think this could be done. (Newsprint will be carefully laid over the fingerpainting, rubbed gently, and peeled off to reveal a print.) Review with your students the definition of printing (stamping or pressing an object covered with paint on to a paper. When lifted off, the object leaves a print.) Ask your students how this kind of printing is different. (Paper is put on the stamp rather than the stamp placed on the paper.) Tell them they will fingerpaint on their desk and then make a monoprint (single print) of their fingerpainting.

Procedure:
- Direct each of your students to:

  Decide on two colors of fingerpaint as you distribute and place two blobs of paint on each desk.

  Tell you what color will result by mixing these colors.

  Fingerpaint until satisfied with the picture or design.

  Clean their hands with a paper towel.

  Lay the newsprint on top of the wet fingerpaint.

  Rub gently over the entire paper to lift the print.

  Peel off the paper and hang or lay it to dry.

- Your students should discover that each print is the mirror image of the painting.

- Your students may want to try another painting; add more paint as needed.

- Have your students clean the desk tops with cleanser and a sponge.

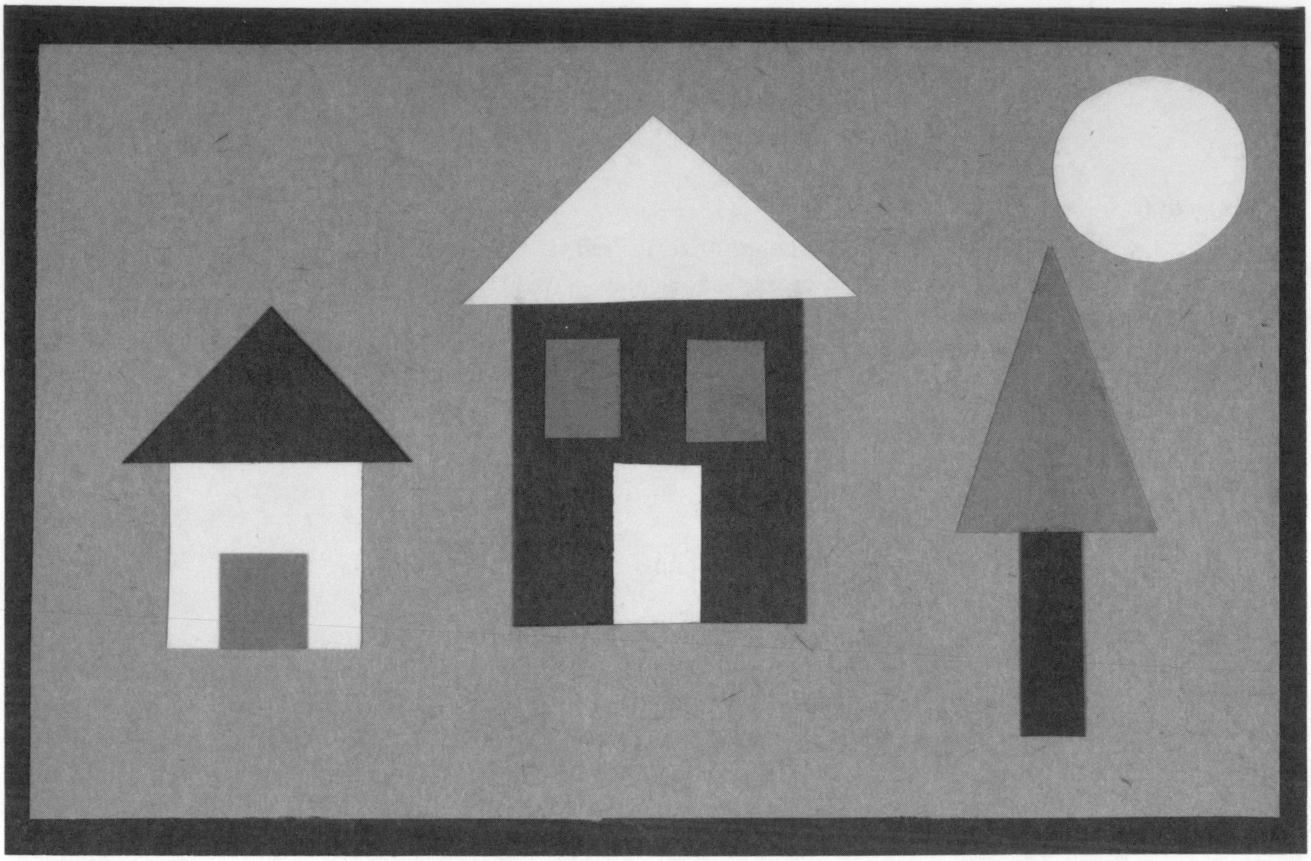

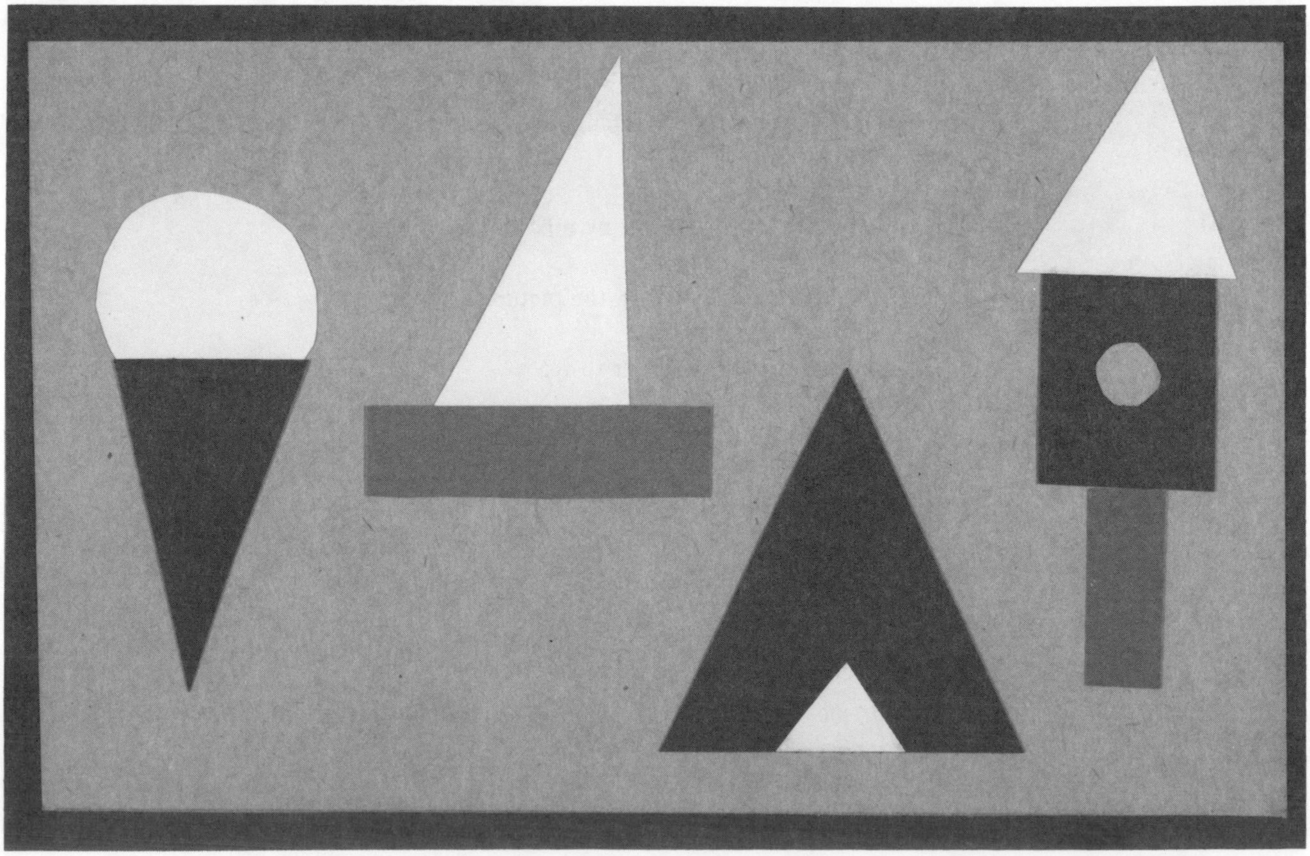

LESSON 34
SHAPES THAT MAKE THINGS

Objective:
- To discover that shapes the students know can be combined with each other to make recognizable objects

Materials:
- Precut shapes   (These are for your use. They should vary in size but all should be of one color.)
- Construction paper, 12″ x 18″
- Construction paper scraps
- Scissors
- Glue

Discussion:
- Use the precut shapes to stimulate ideas. For example:

  Hold up a rectangle and ask, "What shape could be added to this shape to make something?" Strive for several answers such as wagon, train, stop light, and house.

  Hold up two or three shapes and ask, "What could be made with these?" Again strive for several answers.

Tell your students they will be making shape pictures. They may make several objects or a coordinated picture by using combinations of squares, rectangles, circles, ovals and triangles.

Procedure:
- Direct each of your students to:

  Select colored construction paper.

  Cut as many squares, circles, ovals, rectangles, and triangles as desired from construction paper scraps.

  Arrange the shapes on 12″ x 18″ construction paper.

  Glue.

Illustrations:
- John J. Reiss, SHAPES, (Scarsdale, New York: Bradbury Press, Inc. 1974)

- Sharon Lerner, SQUARE IS A SHAPE, (Minneapolis, Minnesota: Lerner Press, 1974)

  These books show shapes placed together to form familiar objects.

LESSON 35
FALL TREES — SPONGE PRINTING

Objectives:
- To become aware of a tree's texture and color
- To discover more about printing

Materials:
- Small cubes of sponge
- Pincher clothespins for handles
- Tempera paint in fall colors
- Aluminum pie tins
- Paper towels
- Newsprint

Discussion:
- If possible take your class outdoors by a tree. Have the children feel the bark. Ask them questions such as:

  What color is the trunk?

  Notice the weathered color of the raised part of the bark and the darker color of the recessed areas. Point out any moss colors.

  Did you think a tree trunk and branches were just brown?

  Did you ever believe a tree trunk had so many colors?

  Does the trunk feel smooth or rough?

  In the fall we get all colors of leaves; how many colors do you see?

Procedure:
- Direct each of your students to:

  Draw the trunk and branches of a tree without the leaves.

  Color this with crayon, remembering the colors and texture of the tree which was just observed.

  Attach a clothespin handle to a sponge.

  Dip the sponge in the tempera and press it on the paper. Use different sponges for different colors.

Illustration:
- Joanne Oppenheim, HAVE YOU SEEN TREES, (New York: Young Scott Books, 1967)

  This book stresses really looking at a tree and should expand your students' personal observations. It is exciting to your sense of sound as well as your sense of sight.

Suggestion:
- This project can also be done in the spring following a discussion of flowering trees.

LESSON 36
WAX PAPER LEAF BANNERS

Objective:
- To incorporate natural objects into an accidental design

Materials:
- Wax paper (precut into 36″ lengths)
- Yarn for hanging banner, 36″ long
- Leaves, weeds, grasses
- Old crayons
- Potato peelers
- Newspaper
- Scissors
- Iron (several, if possible)

Discussion:
- Ask your students what they think a leaf picture that is partly planned and partly accidental might look like. We know what the planned part will look like (leaf arrangement) but if we add crayon chips we will be surprised by the accidental part (how the crayons will melt and fuse). Show your class an example.

  You may wish to take your students on a nature walk to collect their leaves, weeds, and grasses.

Procedure:
- Direct each of your students to:

  Fold the wax paper in half, matching corners.

  Reopen the wax paper.

  Place the yarn next to the fold leaving equal ends on both sides.

  Tie the yarn ends in a double knot to make a hanger.

  Arrange leaves, weeds, and grasses on the bottom half of the wax paper.

  Shave crayons with a potato peeler and scatter the shavings randomly over the leaves and bare spots.

  Cover the arrangement with the top half of the wax paper.

  Place the composition on several thicknesses of newspaper.

  Cover it with two sheets of newspaper and iron with a warm iron.

  Cut a scalloped bottom edge.

Caution:
- *Your students will need close supervision as they iron their banners.*

- *Some large empty areas must be left in the design for the wax paper to stick together when ironed.*

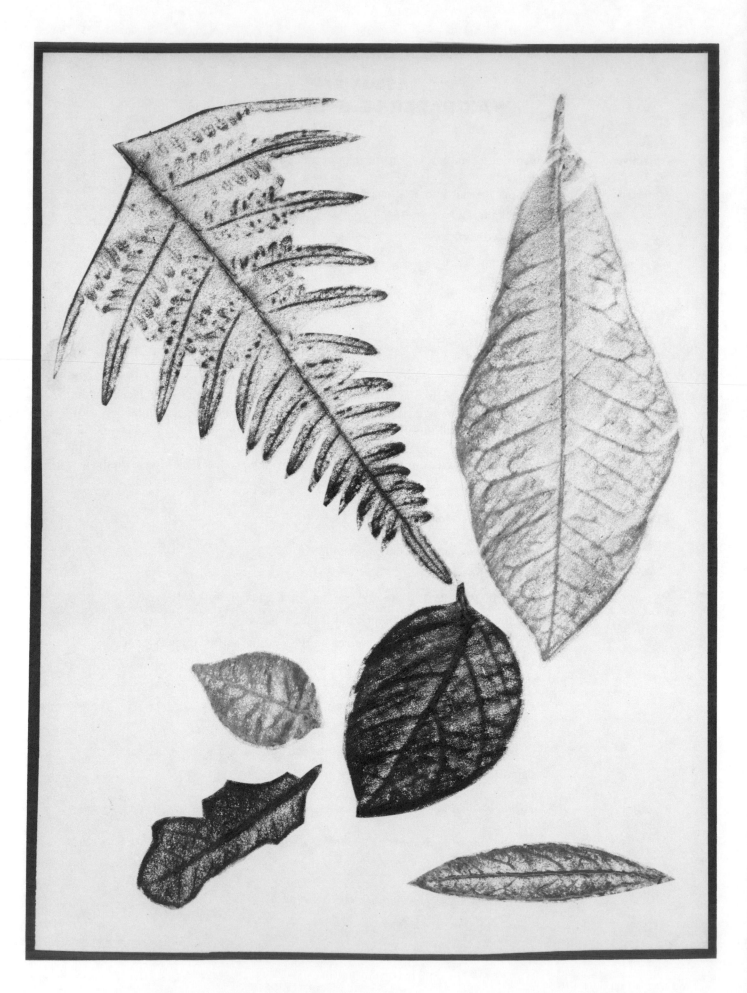

LESSON 37
LEAF COLLAGE — TEXTURE RUB

Objective: • To make your students aware of texture as a characteristic of natural objects

Materials: • Leaves - a wide variety of species and sizes
- Newsprint
- Crayons
- Black construction paper, 9″ x 12″
- Glue
- Scissors

Discussion: • This project would work well in combination with a science unit on leaf identification. Your students should go for a walk to collect a wide variety of leaves. Stress careful collection so that one tree or bush does not lose too many leaves. Upon returning to the classroom, discuss the different shapes of leaves and classify them as to type. Discuss texture (the actual feel of a surface). Some leaves, such as silver maple, have a unique texture. Explain to your students that they will be making a texture rubbing of several leaves and that they will be able to tell the type of leaf used by looking at the resulting rubbing.

Procedure: • Demonstrate the entire procedure before having your students work independently.

   Lay a leaf on a smooth, flat surface with the back side up.

   Cover the leaf with newsprint.

   Hold the paper firmly and rub a crayon over the paper. The image of the leaf will appear.

- Let your students make several rubbings using a variety of colors and leaves.

- Have your students cut out their leaf rubbings, arrange them on the black construction paper and glue when they are pleased with the composition.

- Tell your students that the finished product is a collage (a composition made by gluing various materials to a background).

LESSON 38
SCARY NIGHT PICTURE — HALLOWEEN

Objective:
- To discover that a watercolor wash applied over crayon will not stick to the crayon

Materials:
- White drawing paper, 9″ x 12″
- Crayons
- Watercolor paint box
- Water
- Paper towels

Discussion:
- Have your students discuss what makes Halloween a 'scary' night. List the 'creatures' peculiar to Halloween on the blackboard.

  Define watercolor wash (a thin cover of watercolor paint.) Demonstrate the proper use of watercolors:

  Dip the brush in water.

  Lay the brush on the watercolor square sideways, the back of the brush slightly raised.

  Roll the brush over the square so all sides get covered with color.

  Do not put the point of the brush straight down into the paint. This will cause the bristles to spread and will soon ruin the brush.

  Every time you use a new color rinse the brush.

  Always leave the paintbox clean. If there is any water left in the paint, roll the clean brush over the square to get rid of it.

  Leave the brush clean and pointed.

Procedure:
- Direct each of your students to:

  Color a picture of Halloween night making it as scary as possible.

  Paint over the entire paper, including the crayoned areas, with the paint brush fully loaded with black watercolor.

  Set the picture aside to dry.

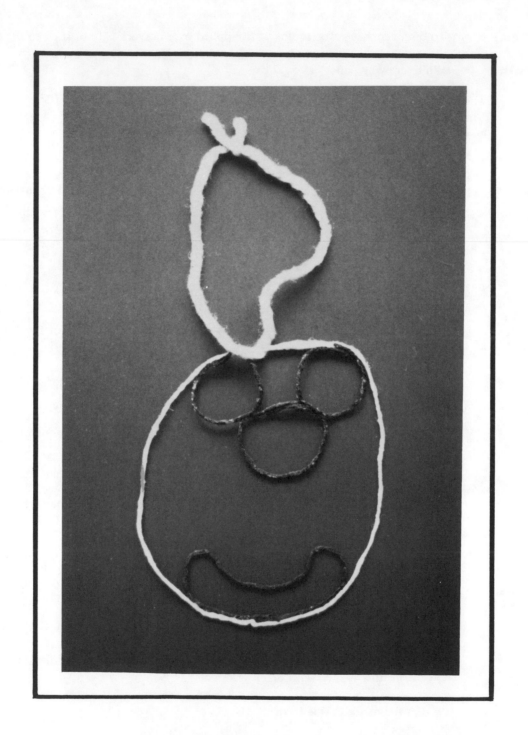

LESSON 39
YARN JACK-O'-LANTERN — LINE DESIGN

Objectives:
- To create a line design
- To make a Halloween mobile

Materials:
- Yarn — orange, black, green, and yellow
- Aluminum foil
- White glue mixed half and half with water
- Shallow containers for glue/water mix

Discussion:
- Ask your students what the difference is between a pumpkin and a jack-o'-lantern. (A jack-o'-lantern has a face.) Have your students suggest different shapes that can be used for eyes, nose and mouth. Tell your students they are going to draw a jack-o'-lantern with yarn; the yarn will take the place of their pencil line.

Procedure:
- Demonstrate the entire procedure before having your students work independently.

  Saturate orange yarn with the glue mixture.

  Remove the excess glue by pulling the yarn between two fingers.

  Place the yarn in the shape of a pumpkin on the aluminum foil. Be sure that the yarn ends overlap and touch for at least two inches.

  Saturate the black or yellow yarn for the mouth, eyes, and nose in the glue mixture and remove the excess glue.

  Arrange the yarn on the foil to make a jack-o'-lantern face, overlapping the ends.

  Set the yarn jack-o'-lantern aside to dry overnight.

  Peel the foil away from the yarn carefully and hang the jack-o'-lantern with green yarn.

Caution:
- *The facial features need to touch each other and/or the edge of the jack-o'-lantern in several places to hold the design together.*

LESSON 40
PATCHWORK DESIGN — WATERCOLOR

Objectives:
- To learn how to work with watercolors
- To create a patchwork design

Materials:
- Bright colored construction paper - 12″ x 18″
- 3″ squares of white drawing paper - 15 per student
- Watercolor boxes
- Water
- Paper towels
- Glue

Discussion:
- Ask your students if they know what a patchwork quilt is. Tell them these got their name because they were made by sewing patches of different materials together. Quilts come in many different patterns; one of the easiest patterns is made with small squares set off by a border.

  Demonstrate the proper use of watercolors:

  Dip the brush in water.

  Lay the brush on the watercolor square sideways, the back of the brush slightly raised.

  Roll the brush over the square so all sides get covered with color.

  Do not put the point of the brush straight down into the paint. This will cause the bristles to spread and will soon ruin the brush.

  Every time you use a new color rinse the brush.

  Always leave the paintbox clean. If there is any water left in the paint, roll the clean brush over the square to get rid of it.

  Leave the brush clean and pointed.

Procedure:
- Direct each of your students to:

  Paint the fifteen squares in varied patterns. The squares may all be different, or a few may be duplicated.

  Allow the squares to dry.

  Arrange the squares on the 12″ x 18″ construction paper, laying three across and five down.

  Leave a space between the squares and around the outside edge for a border.

  Glue down the squares.

Illustration:
- Pictures of patchwork quilts in a variety of patterns.

  These will give your students a sense of historical perspective and show how beauty was incorporated into everyday objects to enhance life.

LESSON 41
SCREEN STITCHERY

Objectives:
- To create an original stitchery
- To improve eye/hand coordination

Materials:
- Wire screen, 9″ x 6″, precut with scissors, with edges enclosed in masking tape to prevent scratches. Screen can be purchased at a hardware store or cut from old window frames.
- Blunt end darning needle - poked through a square of construction paper to prevent rolling
- Scissors
- Yarn

Discussion:
- Ask your students if they know what a stitchery is (a design or picture made by sewing). Talk about sewing and how to safely use a needle. Tell your students they will be sewing with a needle through wire screen.

Procedure:
- Demonstrate the entire procedure before having your students work independently.

  Thread a needle, knotting the end of the yarn so it won't pull through the wire meshes.

  Work with yarn no longer than 18″.

  Sew the yarn through the holes to create a design or a picture. The yarn can go through every mesh like weaving or can skip meshes in any direction. The yarn lines can cross.

  Leave about a 4″ tail of yarn on the back side of the screen when you finish with each color.

  Separate the four-ply yarn into two, two-ply strands, tie the strands in a double knot, and clip the ends.

- Distribute needles, screen, and yarn.

- Let your students stitch a design or a picture using whatever colors they choose.

Suggestion:
- You may want to have parent volunteers present for this project as your students may need help getting started.

Caution:
- *Stress care in working with needles when sitting close together. Do not extend your arm while holding the needle as you do not want to hit anyone with it, particularly not anyone's eye.*

LESSON 42
TISSUE PAPER PINE TREE

Objective:
- To develop eye/hand coordination
- To discover that different shades of color exist in nature

Materials:
- Cones made from green 9″ x 12″ construction paper. (To be made in advance by you)
- Tissue paper, several shades of green, precut into 1″ strips
- Scissors
- Glue
- Shallow pans for glue
- Pencils with erasers

Discussion:
- Have your students observe a pine tree. Point out that the needles on the pine tree are not all the same green, and even those that are the same shade look lighter and darker depending on how the light shines on them. Tell your students they will be making pine trees using several shades of green to make them look more real.

Procedure:
- Demonstrate the entire procedure before having your students work independently.

    Cut the tissue paper strips into 1″ squares.

    Place the tissue square around the eraser end of a pencil and twist. The paper is semi-secured on the pencil.

    Place a small amount of glue in the shallow container.

    Dip the tip of the tissue covered eraser into the glue.

    Place it at the top of the pine tree cone.

    Release the tissue from the pencil.

    Work around the tree, not in a hit or miss fashion, and see that each twisted square is placed tightly against its neighbor on the tree. This will give a soft, full effect.

- Have your students use the varied shades of green randomly.

- Let your students work around the tree until it is completely covered.

Suggestion:
- If you are using this as a holiday gift idea, you might want to add some other colors of tissue paper to represent ornaments.

Caution:
- *This is a long project, but it can easily be stopped at any point and continued at another time.*

LESSON 43
ORANGE PRINT GIFT WRAP

Objective: • To create a printed gift wrap

Materials: • Orange halves
   • Tempera paint
   • Paint containers
   • Brushes
   • Large newsprint
   • Paper towels
   • Newspapers

Discussion: • Re-define printing (placing an inked or painted object firmly on the paper and then carefully lifting it straight up).

Procedure: • Demonstrate the entire procedure before having your students work independently.

   Place a folded newspaper on your desk. The newspaper acts as a slight cushion and helps produce a sharp print.

   Paint an orange half with the tempera.

   Place the orange firmly on the paper and lift off. Several prints can be made from one painting.

   • Have your students work in pairs so they may have two colors of tempera.

   • When the tempera print is dry, one color can be placed on top of another.

Caution: • *If the orange half is very juicy, place it on a paper towel to absorb the excess.*

LESSON 44
SNOWY DAY PICTURE

Note

*Advise parents that your students should wear old clothes for this lesson.
Bleach, if spilled, could ruin good clothes.*

Objective:
- To discover the 'magic' of a new medium

Materials:
- Construction paper, 12″ x 18″, intense colors
- Q Tips
- Liquid bleach
- Shallow containers for bleach

Discussion:
- Ask your students if they have ever seen a blizzard where the wind and the snow made everything look white.

  Talk about bleach. Point out to your students that bleach is poisonous. Ask your students if they know what it does. (It removes colored dye and makes things white.) Tell your students they are going to paint with bleach, and everything they paint will turn white. They are to paint snowy day pictures. The only color besides white on the picture will be the background color. If they paint a house and want the windows to show they will have to outline them and then they will be the color of the background. Tell your students it will look like they are painting with water, but the bleach will turn 'magically' white as it dries, just as the snow turns the world 'magically' white.

Procedure:
- Direct each of your students to:

  Draw a snowy day picture using a Q Tip dipped in bleach.

- Warn your students not to spill any bleach on their clothes as it will take the color out of them just as it will take color out of their papers.

Caution:
- *Before having your students do this project you should try the bleach on the paper to be used. Some paper bleaches out much more completely than others.*

LESSON 45
CUT OUT, STAND UP FAMILIES

Objectives:
- To develop cutting, pasting and drawing skills
- To solve a construction problem

Materials:
- Construction paper
- Pencils
- Glue
- Scissors
- Wallpaper samples
- Yarn

Discussion:
- Ask questions to increase your students' awareness of differences in family members. For example:

  How many people are in a family?

  Do all families have the same members?

  Who is the tallest?

  What color hair and eyes do each have?

Procedure:
- Direct each of your students to:

  Draw every member of their family.

  Cut out each drawing.

  Add hair, facial features, and clothes to each figure using wallpaper, yarn, construction paper, and crayons.

  Make each figure stand up. Allow each student to solve this problem alone.

Suggestion:
- This art project would fit well with a social studies unit on the family.

I am an old fashioned lady with a big long skirt. I am bowing to my partner as I dance.

LESSON 46
BLOB PAINTING — ACCIDENTAL DESIGN

Objective:
- To stretch the imagination
- To have art be the stimulus for a creative writing experience

Materials:
- Blue construction paper, 9″ x 12″
- White tempera paint
- Spoons
- Paper towels

Discussion:
- Take your students outside to observe clouds. (Having them stretch out on their backs works best.) Talk about what they 'see' in the clouds. Tell your students that their imagination helps them see things in many different ways.

Procedure:
- Demonstrate the entire procedure before having your students work independently.

  Fold the paper in half and reopen it.

  Spoon a blob of tempera on to one half of the paper.

  Refold the paper again.

  Rub your hand gently over the paper.

  Open the paper and allow the design to dry.

- Have your students write a story about what they see in their blobs. Stress using their imagination.

- Staple each story to the bottom of the design paper and display.

Illustrations:
- Stephen Lewis, ZOO CITY, (New York: Greenwillow Books, 1976)

  This book imaginatively discovers animals in man made objects.

- Rorschack ink blot test.

  This demonstrates practical application of peoples' ability to see the familiar in abstract shapes.

LESSON 47
FROST PICTURE

Objective:
- To see crystals appear on a winter picture

Materials:
- Epsom salts - 4 oz. dissolved in a pint of *hot* water
- Large brushes
- Light blue construction paper
- Crayons

Discussion:
- Ask your students if they have ever seen frosty window panes. Ask them if they know what makes the frost (water crystals). Tell your students they are each going to color a snowy day picture and then be Jack Frost. Discuss what they might see on a snowy day; for example, snowmen, snowmobiles, drifts, or snowflakes.

Procedure:
- Direct each of your students to:

    Color a complete snowy day picture on blue construction paper.

    Paint over the entire picture with the Epsom salt/water mixture.

- As the picture dries, the frosty crystals will appear.

Suggestion:
- If you do not have really hot water at your school, mix the Epsom salt mixture at home and bring it in a thermos.

    Epsom salt crystals over a bleach picture (Lesson 44) make an effective wintery white picture. The example shown here is of Epsom salt crystals over a bleach picture.

Caution:
- *Advise your students that Epsom salts are poisonous.*

LESSON 48
VALENTINE WEAVING

Objective:
- To further your students' knowledge of weaving
- To create an unusual valentine

Materials:
- White construction paper, 12″ x 18″, precut to form loom. (Fold the paper in half lengthwise. Beginning on the fold, make six cuts, stopping 2″ from the top and spaced so there are seven even strips. Unfold.)

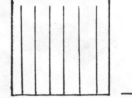
_Fold

- Red construction paper, 12″ x 18″, for heart
- Construction paper strips, 2″ x 12″, for weaving
    Each student needs six.
- Scissors
- Glue

Discussion:
- Review the fact that weaving involves going over and under. Review the procedure for cutting a heart from folded paper. (This should have been mastered before the lesson.)

Procedure:
- Demonstrate the entire procedure before having your students work independently.

    Start at the top of the loom.

    Weave the first strip *over* the first loom strip, *under* the second, *over* the third . . .

    Weave the second strip *under* the first loom strip, then *over* the second, then *under* . . .

    Repeat steps 2 and 3 until all six strips are used.

    Fold the 12″ x 18″ red paper in half and cut out a *large* heart.

    Glue the cut out rectangle over the weaving, matching corners.

    Glue the cut out heart on the back.

LESSON 49
POSITIVE–NEGATIVE (OPPOSITES)

Objective:
- To become aware of how things look different (and yet similar) when reversed
- To create a negative/positive design

Materials:
- Construction paper, 9″ x 12″, varied colors
- Construction paper, 4″ x 9″, varied colors
- Scissors
- Glue

Discussion:
- Have your students discuss opposites. Ask them to name as many opposite word pairs as they can. Tell your students they will make an 'opposite' picture.

Procedure:
- Demonstrate the entire procedure before having your students work independently:

    Take two different colors and sizes of construction paper.

    Cut several small blob-like shapes from both 9″ edges of the 4″ x 9″ sheet. Begin and end cutting on the same edge.

    Glue the smaller sheet down the middle of the large construction paper, matching edges.

    Lay the cut out forms back in their original place.

    Flip the cut out forms back on to the large paper and glue in place.

Caution:
- *Tell your students to keep their forms in order as they cut them.*

LESSON 50
SCRAP WOOD ANIMALS — SCULPTURE

Objective: • To use wood scraps to create an animal sculpture

Materials:
- Scrap lumber - small pieces from home, the lumber yard, or the high school shop class
- Pictures of animals
- Glue
- Tempera paints
- Brushes
- Newspapers

Discussion: • Have your students name all the animals they can. You might list these on the blackboard. Discuss different ways of classifying the animals listed: for example, color, size, habitat, or body coloring. Tell your students they will make an animal sculpture; ask if anyone knows what a sculpture is (a form that can be seen from all sides).

Procedure: • Direct each of your students to:

Choose an animal to make. This can be an imaginary animal or a real one.

Select the wood scraps for the animal.

Experiment with placing the wood scraps together.

Rearrange the wood until the animal assumes a satisfactory form.

Glue the wood pieces individually, making sure that the surface of each piece is covered with a thin layer of glue.

Hold the glued pieces in place until the glue is semi-set (about 5 minutes). Tell your students that they need to hold the wood long enough to let the glue set or their sculpture will collapse.

Set the sculpture aside to dry overnight after all the pieces are glued.

• On the next day have your students cover their desks with newspaper and let them paint their animals with tempera paint. Stress accuracy in colors used.

LESSON 51
3D PAPER SCULPTURE

Objective:
- To explore paper cutting and folding techniques

Materials:
- Construction paper, 12″ x 18″
- Construction paper strips, 1″ x 12″, varied colors
- Glue
- Pencils

Discussion:
- Define sculpture (a form that can be seen from all sides). Tell your students that statues are one kind of sculpture; that is, forms of real people. Tell them they will make a different kind of sculpture - a sculpture of shapes and designs.

  Demonstrate the different ways to cut, fold, and curl paper strips:

  Curl the paper around a pencil for a spiral curl.

  Roll one end *over* in a spiral curl, the other end *under* in a spiral curl.

  Cut one strip in half (6″ long) and cut one end down the middle about 2″. Curl one of the halves forward and the other half backward. Make a ¼″ fold across the other end as a base.

  Make arches by folding ¼″ at one end and gluing it down. Let the paper stretch up to the height you want and glue down the straight end. If you put glue on the top side you get more of a circle. Accordian pleating can also be tried.

  Suggest that some shapes can go through the holes of other shapes or under them.

  Fringe some of the shapes for added interest.

Procedure:
- Direct each of your students to:

  Experiment with varied forms.

  Glue forms to the construction paper.

  Fill the sheet with varied forms.

LESSON 52
PAPER SUNS

Objective: • To explore methods of cutting and folding paper to make interesting edges

Materials: • Construction paper, 12" x 12", various colors
• Construction paper, 9" x 9", various colors
• Construction paper, 6" x 6", various colors
• Scissors
• Crayons
• Glue

Discussion: • Ask your students how to cut a circle from a square. They should be able to say that the corners need to be rounded off. Demonstrate.

Ask your students to suggest ways that the edge of the circle could be cut to make it more interesting; for example, zigzaged, scalloped, fringed, cut away from the edge in sections, or fringed with every other fringe folded out. Demonstrate as your students make suggestions.

Procedure: • Direct each of your students to:

Select three different colors of paper, one of each size.

Cut three circles by rounding off the corners.

Cut and fold the edges of all three circles.

Color a face on the smallest circle with crayon.

Center and glue the circles on top of each other from small to large.

Illustrations: • Pictures of designs with stylized suns

The sun has been a source of wonder to man since the beginning of time. Early man worshipped the sun.

Suggestion: • These make a very colorful wall display. The caption could be "Let the sun shine in."

LESSON 53
MULTIPLE SQUARES — DESIGN

Objective: • To use multiple sizes of a single shape to create a design

Materials: • Construction paper, 9" x 12", all colors
• Construction paper, 5" x 5", all colors
• Scissors
• Glue

Discussion: • Define design (arranging shapes or colors on a paper so they make a pleasing pattern).

Tell your students they will be making a design using many squares. Have them look around the classroom to find examples of several squares placed together in a pattern; for example, window panes, floor tiles, or checked material.

Procedure: • Demonstrate the entire procedure before having your students work independently.

Cut in ¼" from the edge of the 5" x 5" square.

Cut all around the square.

Cut in the same way around the resulting solid square.

Cut progressively smaller outline squares until a solid square approximately ½" x ½" remains.

Arrange the outline squares and the small solid square on the large construction paper in a pleasing pattern.

Glue.

Illustration: • Rene Parola, OPTICAL ART, THEORY AND PRACTICE, (New York: Beekman House, 1969) pp. 72, 76, 110.

The pictured examples are variations on the exercise your students have just completed.

Suggestion: • This project may also be used with other shapes; circles, triangles, and rectangles work equally as well as squares.

LESSON 54
WALL HANGING — WEAVING

Objective: • To discover that different materials can be woven together to create variety and interesting texture in a wall hanging

Materials: • Construction paper, 12″ x 18″, for loom
• Varied precut materials for weaving—strips of material cut with pinking shears, ribbons, yarn, construction paper, wall paper, reeds, wheat, or any straight, 'natural' materials
• Yarn
• Paper punch
• Scissors

Discussion: • Talk about what a wall hanging is (something to hang on the wall that is not a painting and is not framed); for example, banners, macrame, or weavings.

Discuss what would make a woven wall hanging interesting to look at. Some suggestions are different colors, different widths of weft (the material woven through the loom) or different textures.

Procedure: • Demonstrate the entire procedure before having your students work independently.

Fold the 12″ x 18″ construction paper in half lengthwise to make your loom.

Make six cuts, beginning on the fold. Stop 2″ from the top. Space the cuts so there are seven even strips.

Select varied materials to weave.

___ Fold

Weave over, under, over, under in the first row.

Weave under, over, under, over in the second row.

Repeat these two rows until the loom is filled.

Vary the materials woven next to each other. Ends can extend beyond the loom.

Fill the loom.

Punch a hole in the top of the hanging with a paper punch.

Thread a piece of yarn through the hole and tie the ends in a double knot to make a hanger.

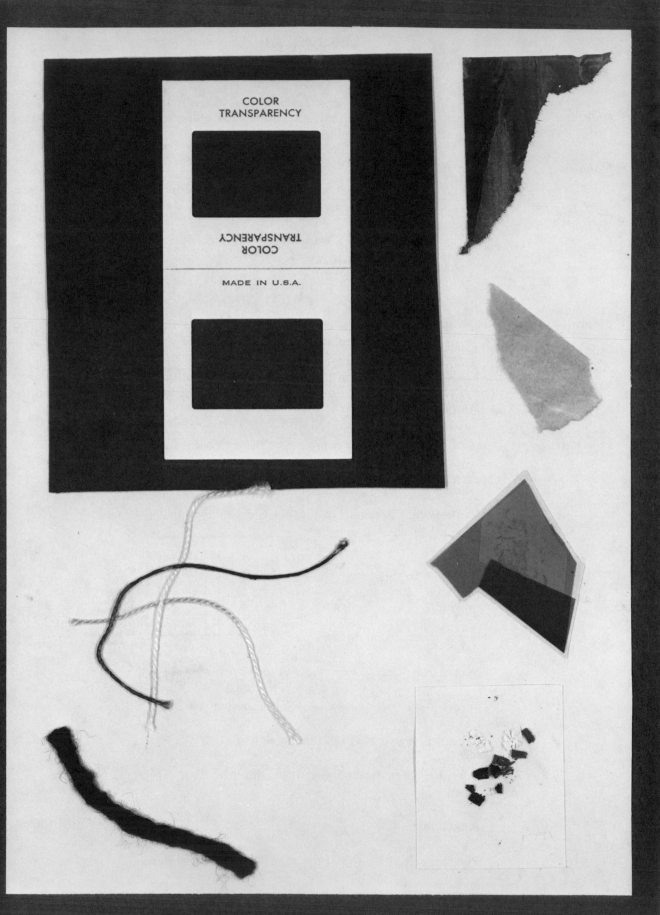

LESSON 55
STUDENT–MADE SLIDES

Objective:
- To discover how unrelated objects placed together can create an interesting design
- To discover that unplanned movement creates interest

Materials:
- Book: Janice Lovoos, DESIGN IS A DANDELION, (San Carlos, California: Golden Gate Junior Books, 1966)
- 36mm color transparency folders (can be purchased at a camera shop)
- Thin, clear plastic cut so it can be folded in half and fit into the transparency folder (The plastic used for overhead projector transparencies works well.)
- Masking tape
- Miscellaneous tiny scraps – for example: yarn, lace, cellophane, twine, or tissue paper
- Old color crayons
- Potato peeler to whittle off color crayon chips
- Scissors
- Rubber cement
- Slide projector and screen

Discussion:
- Ask your students what they think a design is before defining it for them (a pattern or arrangement of shapes).

  Read aloud to the class *Design is a Dandelion* by Janice Lovoos.

Procedure:
- Demonstrate the entire procedure before having your students work independently.

  Select several scraps.

  Place the scraps on the clear plastic.

  Fold the plastic in half over the scraps.

  Place the folded plastic in the transparency folder.

  Seal the edges of the folder with masking tape to make a slide.

  Place the slide in the projector and view.

Suggestions:
- Crayon chips will melt and rubber cement will boil when left in front of the projector light for a short while. This creates unplanned movement in the design. An old fashioned side-by-side projector may work better than a carousel for this project.

  This is a good project to use (after having tried it once) as a program for parents.

LESSON 56
SPRING MURAL — GROUP PROJECT

Objective:
- To work together
- To create a mural

Materials:
- Construction paper
- Pencils
- Scissors
- Glue
- One sheet of blue wrapping paper, 12' long
- Reference books and pictures of animals, insects, birds, and flowers

Discussion:
- Define a mural (a long wall decoration). Ask your students for suggestions about what could be included in a mural about Spring. List the students' suggestions on the blackboard. The following should be included: flowers, grass, birds, butterflies, bugs, trees, and clouds. Tell your students they will each make one thing from every category.

Procedure:
- Direct each of your students to:

    Decide which category to work on first.

    Look at the reference pictures for ideas.

    Draw the picture on construction paper and cut it out.

    Use paper techniques such as fringing, folding, and scalloping.

    Glue the finished picture on the blue background paper which has been taped on the hall wall.

    Choose another category and follow the procedure above.

- You might want to divide your students into groups to work on large objects like trees and clouds.

Illustration:
- Gene Zion, REALLY SPRING, (San Francisco: Harper Row Publications, Inc., 1956)

Suggestions:
- This project is a long one and can be done one category at a time over several days.

- Other ideas for murals would be a circus, a space flight, a farm, a city, or a different season of the year.

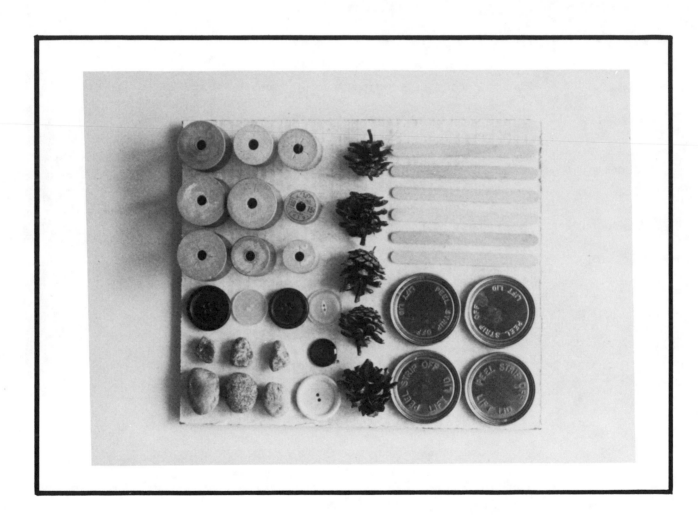

LESSON 57
FOUND OBJECT PATCHWORK COLLAGE

Objective:
- To group similar textured objects
- To create a patchwork collage

Materials:
- Found objects you and your students have collected; for example, spools, buttons, popsicle sticks, acorns, pine cones, seeds, pebbles, bottle caps, spaghetti, or jar lids
- Cardboards for backgrounds - sides of cardboard boxes work well
- Glue
- Rulers
- Pencils

Discussion:
- Define a collage (a composition made by gluing various materials to a background). Define found objects (any object 'found' on a walk or in a certain place. They can be used for printing or in an art composition.).

  Review with your students the idea that a patchwork quilt got its name because it was made by sewing patches of different materials together. Tell your students they will be making a patchwork design using found objects; see how they think this could be done.

  You may want to schedule a walk to collect objects for the project.

Procedure:
- Direct each of your students to:

  Divide the cardboard background into several rectangular areas using a ruler and a pencil. These pencil lines will be only a general guide for arranging objects in the design.

  Arrange the found objects by grouping them within the penciled areas; each area will contain only one type of object.

  Fill each area.

  Arrange the design until a pleasing effect is achieved.

  Glue and allow to dry thoroughly.

Suggestion:
- Collages can be spray painted. This emphasizes the different shapes and textures present and eliminates color differences.

LESSON 58
TISSUE PAPER COLLAGE

Objective:
- To discover how overlapping tissue paper can create color variations
- To utilize the transparent quality of glue covered tissue paper with light to create a stained glass effect

Materials:
- Newsprint, 9″ x 12″
- Plastic food wrap
- Glue and water mixed half and half
- Brushes
- Containers for glue/water mixture
- Tissue paper scraps, all colors

Discussion:
- You should have small pieces of different colored tissue paper as well as one sheet each of yellow and red construction paper for this demonstration. Hold the red and yellow tissue paper against the window; move them so they overlap and create orange. Ask your students what happened; yellow and red made orange. Hold the red and yellow construction paper against the window and move them so they overlap. Ask your students what happened—nothing. Ask them why. Your students should realize that the *light* shining through the tissue paper is what makes the tissue colors fuse. Tissue paper is *translucent* which makes it like stained glass. Construction paper is *opaque* and the light does not shine through it.

Procedure:
- Demonstrate the entire procedure before having your students work independently.

    Lay the plastic wrap on top of the newsprint so that it overlaps. The newsprint is only used as a guide for size. The collage is to be done on the plastic wrap.

    Paint the glue/water combination on the plastic wrap.

    Select several colors of tissue paper.

    Tear the tissue into irregular shapes.

    Lay the tissue paper pieces on the glue covered plastic wrap so they overlap. This makes a solid sheet of tissue and creates color variations. Some of the colors will run. This gives added interest.

    Paint over each piece of tissue with the glue/water mix as it is laid on the plastic wrap.

    Cover the complete 9″ x 12″ area and set aside to dry overnight.

- The next day have your students gently peel the tissue away from the plastic wrap.

- Display the collages in a window.

LESSON 59
BURLAP STITCHERY

Objective:
- To create an original stitchery using running, satin, star, split, and whipped stitches

- To improve eye/hand coordination

Materials:
- Burlap, precut into 6″ x 9″ pieces, edges enclosed in masking tape to prevent raveling
- Burlap, miscellaneous sizes, for students to practice stitches on
- Small embroidery hoops (optional, but highly desirable)
- Pictures of animals and bugs
- Yarn
- Scissors
- Newsprint, 6″ x 9″
- Reference book showing embroidery stitches, for your use
- Blunt end darning needles

Discussion:
- Ask your students if they know what a stitchery is (a design or picture made by sewing). Talk about sewing with a needle; *stress safe usage*. Demonstrate how to thread a needle and knot the end of the yarn so it will not pull through material. Distribute needles, yarn, and practice pieces of burlap to your students. Demonstrate the running, satin, star, split, and whipped stitches; have your students try each stitch as you show them how.

Procedure:
- Direct each of your students to:

  Choose an animal or a bug for the stitchery.

  Make a practice drawing on the 6″ x 9″ newsprint.

  Draw the picture on the burlap with a ball point pen using the picture on the newsprint as a guide.

  Decide which stitches to use, using as many of the practiced stitches as possible.

  Select yarn colors.

  Sew the picture.

Illustration:
- Nik Krevitsky, STITCHERY ART AND CRAFT, (New York: VanNostrand Reinhold Co., 1966) pp. 44-49.

  Illustrations of students' work should be of interest to your students when they have just completed a similar project.

Suggestion:
- This lesson might best be used on two days — one for practice and one for the final stitchery. Your students could be urged to practice their stitches at home. A note of explanation and directions to parents would insure cooperation.

- You may want to have parent volunteers help with this project.

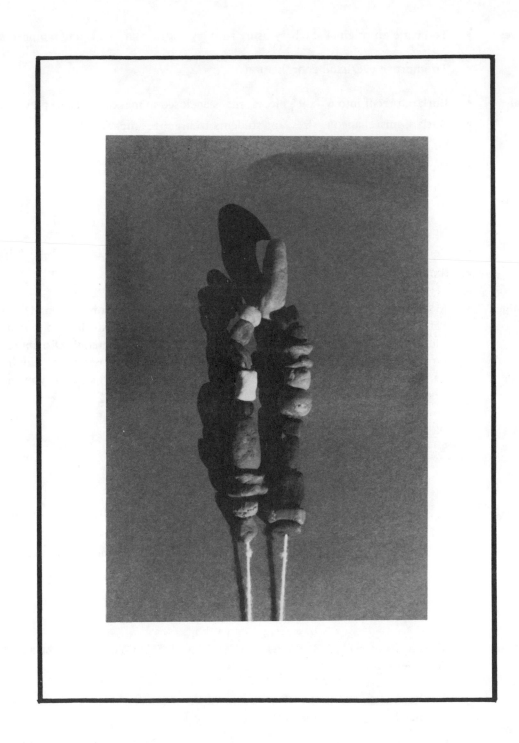

LESSON 60
PLAY DOUGH BEADS

Objective
- To make beads in a variety of shapes
- To learn the difference between repeat and random patterns

Materials:
- Play dough: Make this in advance. One recipe makes approximately 75 average size beads. The dough should be smooth, not crumbly. If the dough gets crumbly, wet hands with a little water and knead; if it gets too wet, add a little flour and knead. Store the play dough in a plastic bag.

  Play dough recipe:
  1 cup flour
  ½ cup salt
  ⅓ cup water

- Thin knitting needles
- Yarn
- Blunt pointed darning needles poked through small pieces of construction paper so they will not roll
- Aluminum foil
- Water colors

Discussion:
- Ask your students what forms would make interesting beads for a necklace; i.e., spheres, cubes, cylinders, flat circles, flat squares, hearts, and flower shapes. Demonstrate with play dough as suggestions are made.

  Talk about how beads could be strung in a repeat pattern (round, square, round, square, . . .) or in a random pattern (round, oval, square, rectangle, . . .).

Procedure:
- Direct each of your students to:

  Shape beads from the play dough.

  Pierce each bead with a knitting needle to make a hole large enough to string yarn through. If the holes are not big enough, beads will break when strung.

  Lay the beads on foil and set them aside to dry. Beads will take at least three days to air dry. They should be turned over on the second day so that the side next to the foil gets exposed to the air.

  Paint the beads with watercolors when they have dried completely.

  Set the beads on foil to dry. This will take at least an hour.

  Turn the beads once for uniform drying.

  Thread a needle with yarn.

  Knot the thread about 6″ from the end.

  String the beads, leaving 6″ of yarn at the end. This allows two ends for tying the necklace around the neck.

Suggestion:
- Spraying beads lightly with clear plastic will prevent color from rubbing off.

Caution:
- *Show your students how to safely handle needles.*

ALL CHILDREN CREATE

Lessons:

Level 3

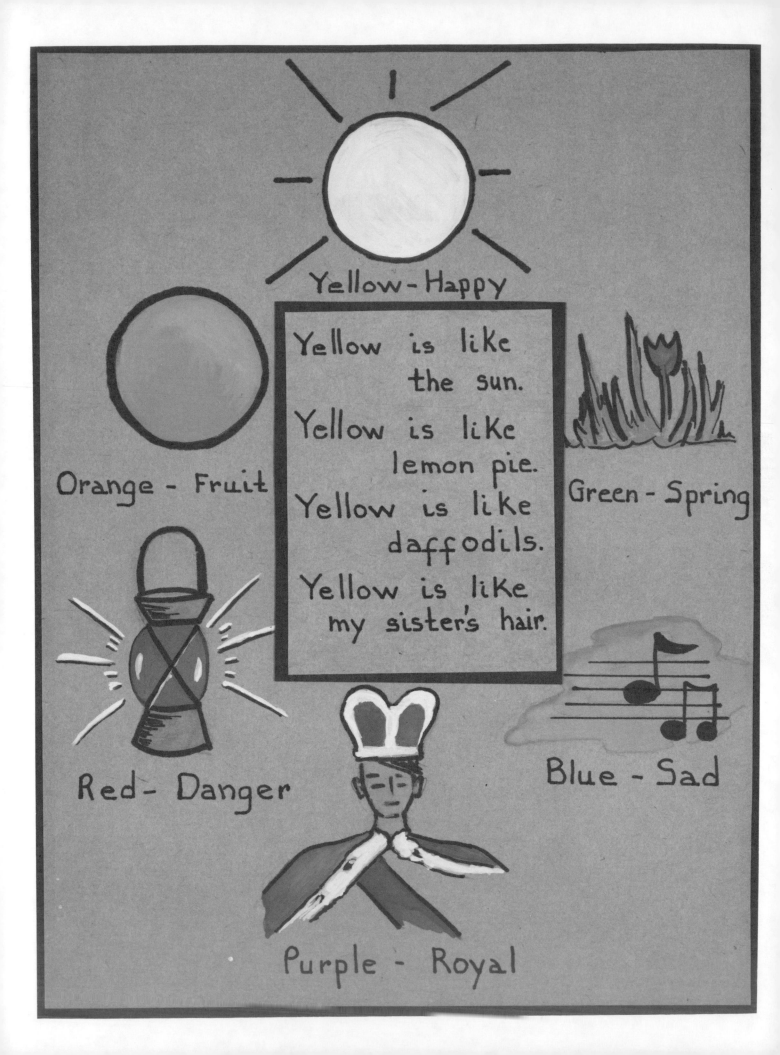

LESSON 61
COLOR AWARENESS IN OUR LANGUAGE

Objective:
- To realize how color is used to describe moods, situations, and emotions
- To write a color poem

Materials:
- Paper
- Pencils

Discussion:
- Name a color and ask your students what it makes them think of or how it makes them feel. Possible answers include:

Blue	Sad (I've got the blues)
Red	Danger (red warning signs)
Yellow	Coward (He's yellow)
	Happy (sunshine)
Black	(is beautiful)
	Death (somber)
Green	Rebirth (Spring)
Orange	Food (the fruit)
Purple	Royal
White	Purity

When they are done discussing the colors, you should explain the rareness of purple dyes in ancient times. This made anything purple very expensive and so this color was reserved for royalty. Tell your students they are going to write a group poem. Have the group select a color they would like to use for a poem.

Procedure:
- Direct each of your students to:

    Take a piece of paper and a pencil.

    Write one sentence about the chosen color.

    Start the sentence with Yellow is . . . , or Yellow is like . . .

- Collect all the papers. Read the lines aloud as one poem.

- Repeat the procedure using different colors.

Illustrations:
- Ed Emberley, GREEN SAYS GO, (Boston, Mass.: Little Brown & Co., 1968)
- Ann McGovern, BLACK IS BEAUTIFUL, (New York: Four Winds Press, 1969)

    These books further expand on how color expresses moods, emotions, and situations.

Suggestion:
- The poems should be typed on a ditto and distributed to all of your students at a later time. They also make a nice bulletin board display framed in appropriate colors.

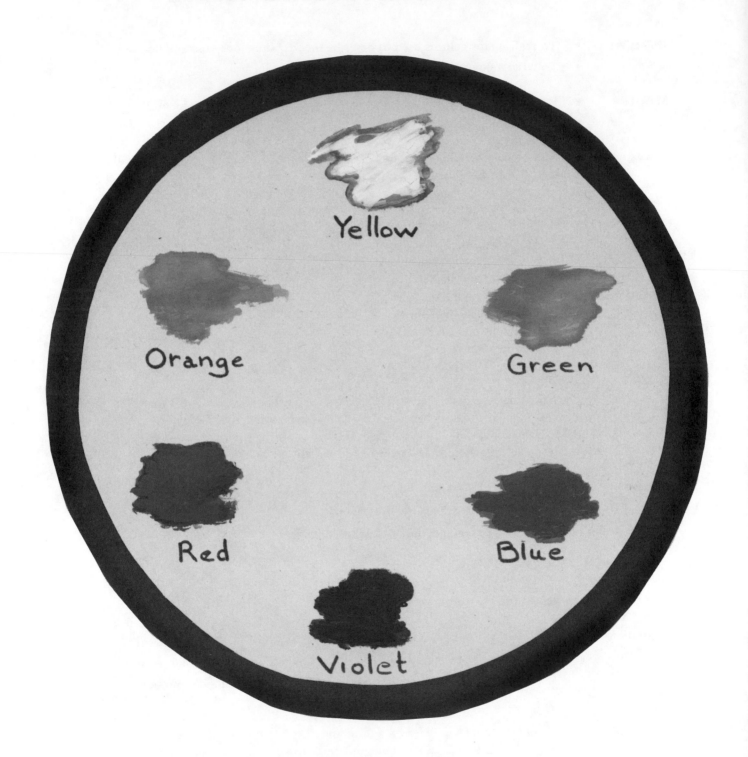

LESSON 62
COLOR AWARENESS

Objective:
- To understand that the color wheel is a tool
- To learn the terms primary and secondary colors

Materials:
- White paper
- Brushes
- Tempera paint (red, yellow, and blue)
- Water

Discussion:
- Ask your students to name the three *primary* colors (red, yellow, and blue) and explain that all colors are made from them.

  Use white drawing paper and paint on a blob of each primary color. The three blobs should roughly designate a triangle: yellow at the top, like the sun; red at the lower left; blue at the lower right.

  Tell your students you are now ready to make the *secondary* colors. As you mix them make a point of working with a clean brush to keep the colors bright.

  Ask your students how to make orange (red plus yellow). Mix red and yellow paint in the paint tray and put a blob of orange between the red and yellow blobs on the drawing paper. Tell your students you are placing it in this position because the color wheel indicates that red and yellow make orange.

  Repeat the procedure for purple (red plus blue).

  Repeat the procedure for green (yellow plus blue).

Procedure:
- Direct each of your students to:

  Make a color wheel.

LESSON 63
DESIGN WITH PRE-CUT SHAPES

Objective:
- To use pre-cut shapes to create a balanced design

Materials:
- Construction paper, pre-cut in many varied shapes, colors and sizes
- Colored construction paper, 12″ x 18″, for background
- Glue

Discussion:
- Discuss balanced design (a design that doesn't look too heavy or crowded in one place and too light or empty in another).

  Dark colors look heavier than light colors. Squares look heavier than circles or triangles of a similar size. One large object looks heavier than several small objects that are clustered or separated. You should demonstrate these concepts.

  Tell your students they are going to make a balanced design.

Procedure:
- Direct each of your students to:

  Choose several shapes.

  Arrange the shapes on a background paper to achieve a balanced and interesting design. Shapes may overlap.

  Glue the shapes to the background paper.

- Have the class analyze all the designs.

Caution:
- *Be positive in this critique. There are good things to be found in all of the designs. The purpose is not to crush students' feelings, but to have your students learn about the concepts discussed. You should say, "What do you like about this design?"*

LESSON 64
LEAF PRINT

Objective:
- To learn more about printing
- To make a pleasing composition

Materials:
- Construction paper, 9″ x 12″
- Tempera paint
- Brushes
- Leaves
- Paper towels

Discussion:
- This project should be done in the fall. Have your students discuss the similarities and the differences in a variety of leaves. The elements of shape, color, and size should be mentioned.

  Review the difference between painting and printing. (Printing is stamping or pressing an object covered with paint on to a paper. When lifted off, the object leaves a print.) Your students should try to determine which parts of a leaf will print.

Procedure:
- Direct each of your students to:

  Choose several leaves.

  Select paper and paint colors.

  Paint the back side of a leaf lightly with tempera.

  Press the leaf on to the paper.

  Lift the leaf off carefully. Two or three prints can be made from one painting. If too much paint gets on the leaf, blot it with a paper towel.

  Clean the brush before using another color of paint.

  Use the same procedure for each leaf.

- Let your students place the leaves in an arrangement of their own choosing. Prints may overlap.

Suggestion:
- This project would work well with a science unit. A nature hike could be taken to identify local plant life and to collect leaves.

LESSON 65
HANGING WEED POT — CLAY

Objective:
- To make a weed pot using the slab technique
- To learn what intaglio printing is

Materials:
- Clay - if unavailable, play dough (page 137) can be substituted successfully
- Weeds for imprinting
- Dowel
- Wax paper
- Toothpicks
- Yarn

Discussion:
- Tell your students what a slab is (a piece of clay that is flat, broad, and fairly thick). A ball of clay is rolled out in the same way as cookie dough. The resulting slab can be cut, folded, or joined to another slab to make a form. A simple method of joining slabs is to pinch the edges together as you would crimp a pie crust. Tell your students they are going to make a hanging slab weed pot out of clay and they are going to imprint the pattern of a weed in the slab. This is called intaglio printing (a design or figure carved or engraved below the surface).

Procedure:
- Demonstrate the entire procedure before having your students work independently:

  Wedge a lump of clay six times. This is like kneading bread.

  Form the clay into a ball.

  Decide on a shape for your weed pot. Some possibilities are a cylindrical shape, a folded-over form, or two shapes cut separately and crimped together.

  Roll the clay with a dowel until it is about ¼" thick.

  Place a weed on wax paper. Lift the clay and lay it on top of the weed. Roll over the clay with the dowel several times to make an imprint.

  Pull the wax paper and the weed away from the clay. If some parts of the weed stick in the clay, use a toothpick to dislodge them.

  Crumple a piece of wax paper to form the inside space of the weed pot as the clay is folded or joined. The paper should remain in until the clay hardens, then it should be removed. Roll a cylinder of construction paper, cover it with wax paper, and use it as a form to roll the clay around if you are making a cylindrical pot.

  Use your thumb and a finger to crimp the edges.

  Poke two holes at the top of the pot with a pencil.

  Set the pot aside to dry.

  Check with the high school art teacher for directions about bisque firing in a kiln.

  Thread yarn through the holes, add weeds, and hang.

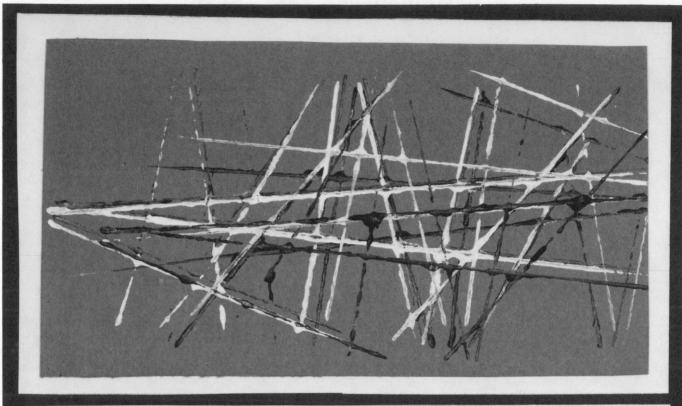

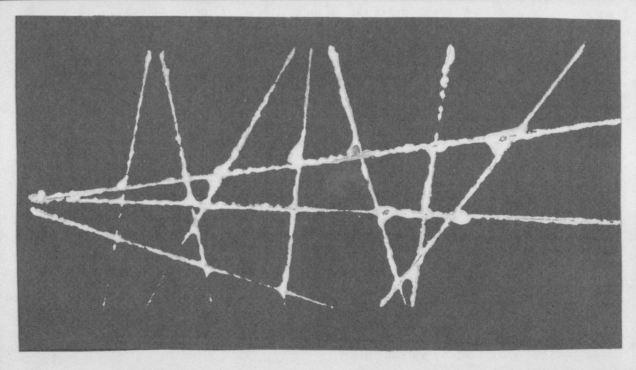

LESSON 66
STRING PRINT — LINE DESIGN

Objective:
- To discover a new method of printing
- To explore possible variations from one printing design

Materials:
- Small blocks of wood
- String
- Tempera paint
- Brushes
- Masking tape
- Construction paper, 9" x 12"
- Newsprint
- Newspapers

Discussion:
- Define printing (stamping or pressing an object covered with paint on to a paper. When lifted off the object leaves a print.). Tell your students the print they will make is a line design. Line is one of the elements of art.

Procedure:
- Direct each of your students to:

  Take a block of wood.

  Wind string around it in a random fashion.

  Fasten the string ends on the back of the block with masking tape.

  Cover the desk with several layers of newspapers. This acts as a cushion to make a sharp print.

  Lay newsprint on the newspapers.

  Paint the string with tempera paint.

  Press the string on the newsprint and lift off. Each painting will make four or five prints.

  Experiment with overlapping prints, and with running prints vertically as well as horizontally.

  Rinse the string and the brush and print a second color over the first.

- Have your students mount two examples of their prints on construction paper; one example should be the single, original pattern, the other should be their favorite variation.

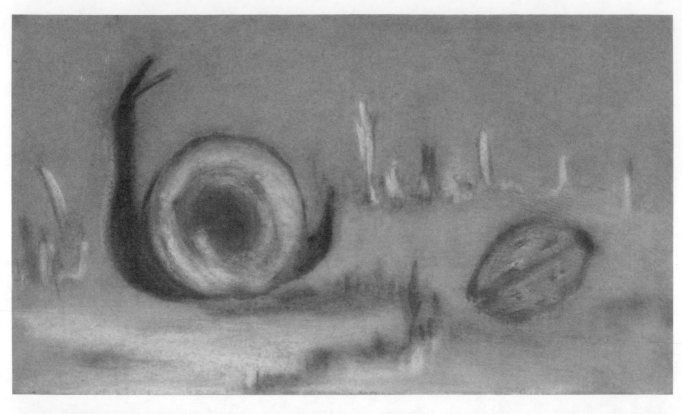

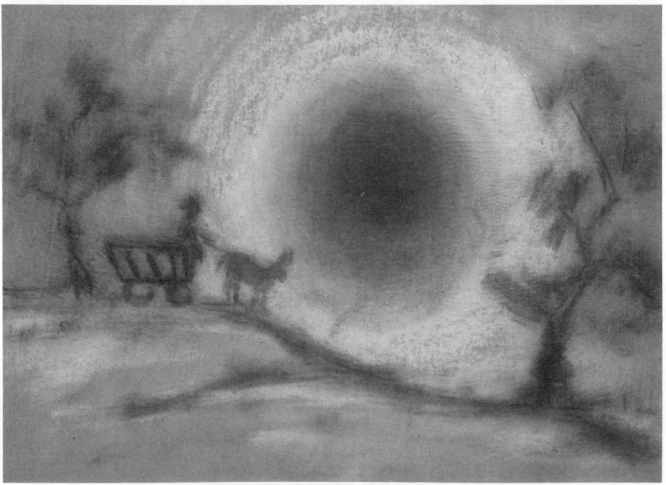

LESSON 67
CHALK PICTURE

Objective: • To discover different ways to use chalk

Materials: • Colored chalk
• Newsprint
• White drawing paper, 12″ x 18″

Discussion: • Demonstrate on the blackboard or on a large sheet of paper as you discuss the ways chalk can be used:

Chalk held and used as a pencil makes a sharp line.

Chalk turned on its side and pulled down the page makes a soft, broad line.

Chalk held as a pencil can be used for outlining, making objects stand out sharply.

Chalk can be applied lightly, giving a soft look, or applied heavily, giving a more definite effect.

Chalk laid on its side and twisted in a circle makes a solid circle that is darker in the center.

Chalk laid on its side and moved in a 'S' curve makes a thick and thin line.

Chalk can be blended. Using the side of the chalk, two colors can be overlapped. Rubbing the overlapped area with a finger blends the colors to make a soft edge.

Tell your students they are going to draw a chalk picture or design after they have practiced using the chalk.

Procedure: • Direct each of the students to:

Practice all of the chalk techniques on newsprint.

Choose a topic for a picture.

Sketch a picture with light colored chalk on the white drawing paper.

Use all the chalk techniques that have been discussed in the drawing.

• You may suggest a topic for a picture based on the season of the year or something that the students are studying; for example, rainbows, flowers, fish, or water.

Illustration: • Arnold Spilka, PAINT ALL KINDS OF PICTURES, (New York: Scholastic Book Service, 1963)

Reading this book aloud could lead to a discussion of the kind of picture each student drew.

Caution: • *This is a purely exploratory lesson.*

LESSON 68
CHALK DRAWING ON WET PAPER

Objective: • To discover how wet paper changes the look of chalk

Materials: • Colored chalk
   • Drawing paper
   • Water
   • Sponges
   • Cleanser

Discussion: • Review and demonstrate the chalk techniques covered in the preceding lesson. Your students will discover that the final effect is different when they work on wet paper as opposed to dry.

Procedure: • Direct each of your students to:

Wet a piece of drawing paper on both sides. Hold the paper under the faucet, let the excess water drip off, then roll the paper in a cylinder to prevent dripping as it is carried back to the desk.

Smooth the paper on to the desk.

Practice with chalk using the techniques discussed and demonstrated.

Wet a second paper and draw a picture or design.

Set the picture aside to dry.

Use a sponge and cleanser for clean up.

Exemplar: • Stanton MacDonald-Wright, "Synchrony in Green and Orange" in Daniel Mendelowitz, A HISTORY OF AMERICAN ART, (New York: Holt, Rinehart and Winston, Inc., 1970) p. 376.

This is an oil painting but it resembles a chalk painting with its shading. Have your students discuss how they could get these effects with chalk.

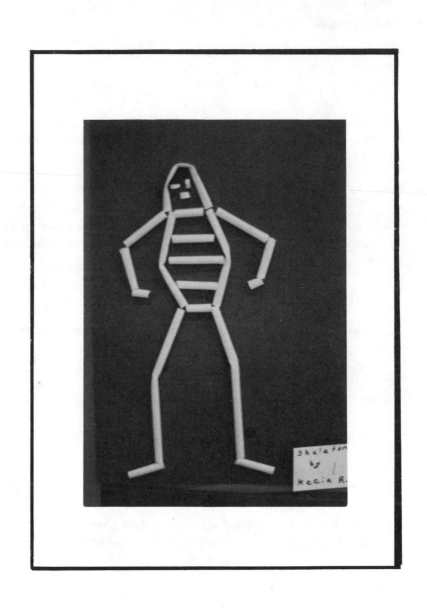

LESSON 69
HALLOWEEN SKELETON

Objective:
- To observe and discuss the body structure and proportions
- To create a bas-relief sculpture

Materials:
- White paper straws
- Black construction paper, 9" x 12"
- White mimeograph paper, 9" x 12"
- Glue
- Scissors
- Skeleton for demonstration

Discussion:
- Use a skeleton model or a paper Halloween skeleton to demonstrate. Ask questions such as:

  Why are the bones of the chest called the rib cage? (Your students should be able to see that these bones go horizontally to enclose the chest.)

  How far down do the arms hang?

  How many bones are there in the upper arm? lower arm? upper leg? lower leg?

  Where does the backbone begin and end? Point out that the neck is part of the backbone. Students are apt to forget the neck when drawing the human body.

  Ask your students if they know what a bas-relief sculpture. (A sculpture which is attached to a flat surface on one side and extends outward on the other. It is two dimensional.) Coins have bas-relief sculpture on them.

Procedure:
- Direct each of your students to:

  Sketch a skeleton on the white mimeograph paper. The drawing should fill the page.

  Cut or bend the straws using the sketch as a guide. The straws are used to represent the bones.

  Arrange the straws on the black construction paper.

  Glue.

LESSON 70
HALLOWEEN MURAL — GROUP PROJECT

Objectives:
- To complete a group project
- To stimulate the imagination

Materials:
- Long sheet of wrapping paper
- Newsprint, 12" x 18"
- Scissors
- Glue
- Construction paper

Discussion:
- Have your students discuss Halloween and all the 'creatures' peculiar to the holiday.

  Define a mural (a long wall decoration).

  Discuss overlapping. Your students should know that objects in front cover up part of the object behind them.

  Tape a long sheet of wrapping paper to a wall in the hall or the room as a background for the mural. Tell your students they are going to make a Halloween mural.

Procedure:
- Direct each of your students to:

  Sketch a scary Halloween creature on newsprint. The drawing should fill the paper.

  Use the newsprint sketch as a guide.

  Cut colored construction paper to make the 'creature'.

  Assemble and glue the 'creature' together.

  Glue the finished creature to the wrapping paper background.

- Tell your students the 'creatures' are to be in a group as though they were waiting to have their picture taken. Stress that the figures will overlap as if some creatures are standing behind others.

- Have your students who finish early add other Halloween details made from construction paper; for example, jack-o-lanterns, bats, a full moon, or a bare tree.

LESSON 71
REPEAT PATTERNS

Objective:
- To create a repeat pattern

Materials:
- Mimeograph paper
- Construction paper, 9" x 12"
- Scissors
- Glue

Discussion:
- Define a repeat pattern (a pattern that occurs over and over and over). Suggest that the panes in a window, or the slats in venetian blinds create a very simple repeat pattern. Ask your students to find other repeat patterns in the room.

Procedure:
- Direct each of your students to:

  Fold a sheet of mimeograph paper in an accordian or fan fold.

  Cut into the paper on all sides of the folded strip. Each cut must go in and come out on the same side.

  Unfold the paper.

  Glue the design on to construction paper.

- If your students wish, they can unfold their papers at any point to see how the designs are progressing.

Illustration:
- Pictures of repeat patterns in everyday things, such as snow fences, row houses, or bricks in a wall, help students become aware of design in their own environment.

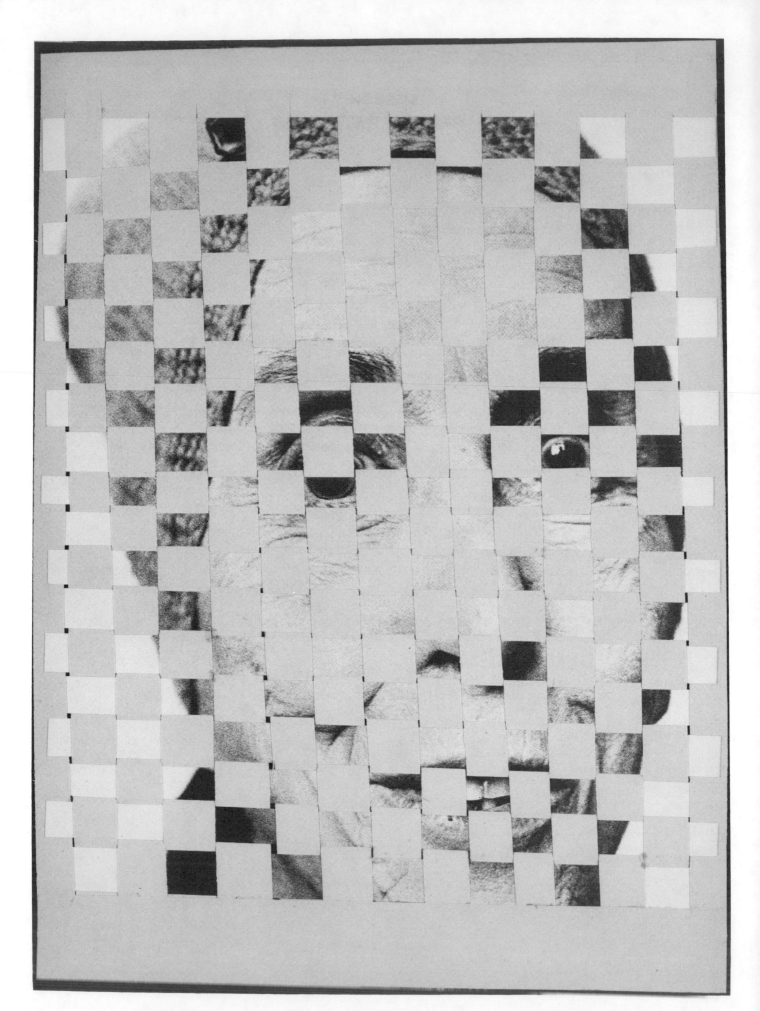

LESSON 72
PAPER WEAVING

Objectives:
- To review weaving terms
- To discover a different weft for weaving

Materials:
- Magazine pictures
- Construction paper (same width as, but about 4" longer than magazine pictures)
- Scissors
- Glue

Discussion:
- Review the terms warp, weft, and loom.
  The *loom* is the thing you weave on.
  The *warp* is the lengthwise thread that is strung on the loom.
  The *weft* is the thread that is woven over and under the warp.

  Review the over/under process of weaving.

Procedure:
- Direct each of your students to:

  Make a loom from construction paper. Starting at the bottom, make several cuts to within 1½" of the top. The resulting strips should be quite thin (about ¼" wide) in order for the weaving to be most effective.

  Select a magazine picture.

  Cut one crosswise strip, ½" wide, from the magazine picture.

  Weave the strip before cutting the next strip. This eliminates confusion.

  Weave the strip over and under, over and under, across the loom.

  Cut a second strip ½" wide, and weave it across the loom, starting under the warp.

  Repeat the two steps above until the picture is woven into the loom. Each weft end can be secured to the loom with a drop of glue.

  Cut a 2" construction paper strip of the same color as the loom.

  Seal the bottom of the weaving by gluing the strip across the bottom of the loom.

Suggestion:
- Pictures cut from the *National Geographic* are particularly good for this project as the colors are excellent and the paper is a good, strong weight.

LESSON 73
CORN HUSK PINE TREE

Note

Corn husks needed for this project should be collected in the fall.

Objective:
- To work with natural materials

Materials:
- Cones, made in advance from 9" x 12" beige construction paper
- Corn husks (husks from two cobs of corn required for each student)
- Scissors
- Bowls for water
- Blunt pointed darning needles
- Glue
- Paper towels
- Rulers

Discussion:
- Talk about corn husk dolls and how natural materials were used in early days because that was all people had.

Procedure:
- Demonstrate the entire procedure before having your students work independently.

    Cut the corn husks in 2" strips across the grain.

    Place the cut pieces in a bowl of water to make them pliable. This takes a few minutes so suggest to your students that they put six pieces in at the start. After they have used three pieces, they should start three more soaking to make the project move smoothly.

    Remove one pliable strip from the water.

    Lay it straight on a paper towel.

    Fringe the strip with a blunt needle:
    Hold the husk uncurled with the left hand.
    Punch the needle through the strip about ½" from the top.
    Pull the needle straight down along the grain.

    Show your students how the husk is inclined to curl inward. You want this inward side to face outwards on your tree allowing it to curl as it dries.

    Lay the fringed piece flat on the desk, the inward side down.

    Place glue thickly on the top edge of the husk.

    Glue the strip to the cone, starting at the bottom. The fringe should be even with the bottom of the cone.

    Work around the cone row by row. The fringe should overlap the preceding row so that all but about ½" is covered.

- At the top, fringe one last piece of husk, roll it tightly around the needle and put it through the tiny hole in the top of the cone.

Illustration:
- Corn husk dolls and pine cone wreaths

    Point out to your students that both examples demonstrate the craft possibilities in natural materials.

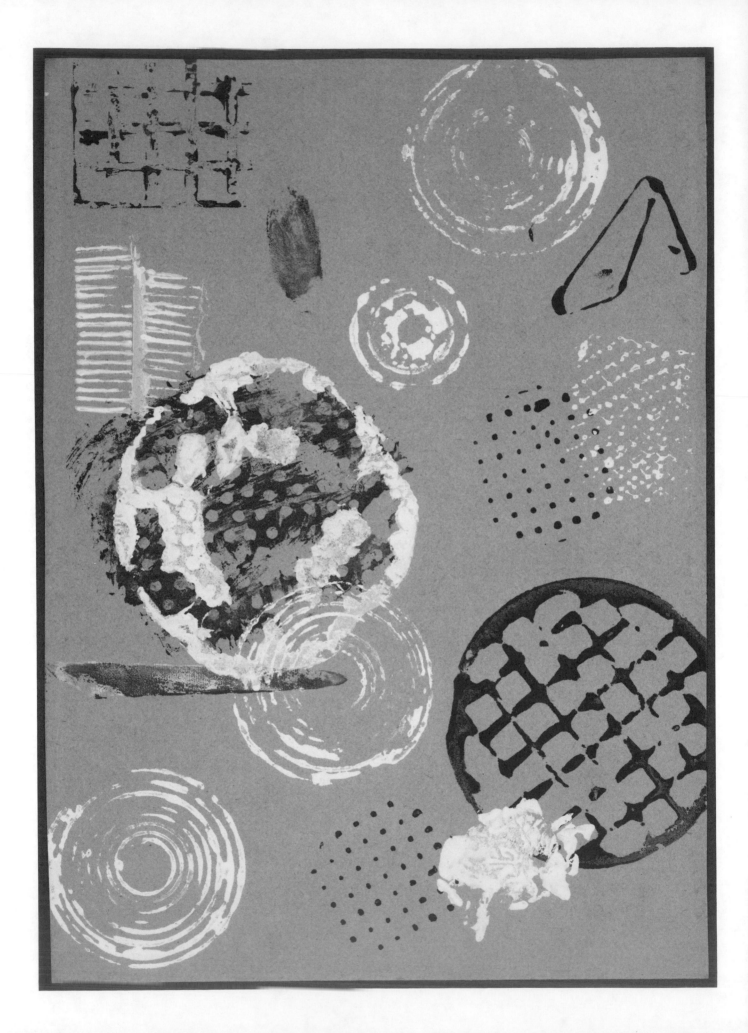

LESSON 74
FOUND OBJECT PRINTED GIFT WRAP

Objectives:
- To create a printed pattern from found objects
- To create a gift wrap

Materials:
- Found objects; bark, kitchen utensils, spools, paper clips, or pine cones
- Tempera paint
- Brushes
- Water
- Newsprint
- Paper towels

Discussion:
- Review the definition of printing (stamping or pressing an object covered with paint on to a paper. When lifted off the object leaves a print.).

  Define found objects (any object 'found' on a walk or in a certain place).

Procedure:
- Demonstrate the entire procedure before having your students work independently.

  Choose a found object.

  Paint the object with tempera.

  Press the painted object firmly on the paper and lift it off. Several prints can be made from one painting.

  Clean the object and the brush before applying a second color.

- Patterns can be overlapped after the first color dries.

- Have your students experiment on a sheet of newsprint before making their actual gift wrap.

LESSON 75
TISSUE PAPER SNOWFLAKES — SYMMETRICAL DESIGN

Objectives:
- To cut a symmetrical shape
- To explore color mixing

Materials:
- Tissue paper
- Scissors
- Circular objects for patterns (plates, lids, cups)
- Paint brushes
- Flair pens
- Salad oil

Discussion:
- Define symmetry (a mirror image that is the same on both sides). Ask your students to name the symmetrical shapes they already know how to cut (hearts and four sided snowflakes). Tell them that today they will cut six sided snowflakes. Real snowflakes are six sided. Remind them that no two snowflakes are exactly alike.

Procedure:
- Demonstrate the entire procedure before having your students work independently.

  Trace a circle pattern on the tissue paper using a flair pen.

  Cut out the circle.

  Fold the circle in half to make a semicircle.

  Fold the semicircle into thirds to make a pie-shaped wedge.

  Cut blob like shapes from each edge of the folded tissue paper making sure that each cut begins and ends on the same edge.

  Open the tissue circle to see the completed snowflake.

- Let your students cut several snowflakes from different colored tissue paper. They can be different sizes.

- Snowflakes are to be applied to a window. An inside window works best as there is no condensation.

- Have each student hold a snowflake against the window and brush over it lightly with salad oil. This will hold the snowflake to the window and also give a translucent effect.

- A second snowflake can be laid over the first. It may not need to be painted as the oil from the first snowflake will soak into it.

- Where the snowflakes overlap, your students will discover a new color.

- Let your students fill the window.

Illustration:
- Marion Walter, THE MAGIC MIRROR BOOK, (New York: Scholastic Book Services, 1975)

  This book demonstrates symmetry through the use of an actual mirror image.

LESSON 76
WINTER MOBILE

Objectives:
- To use a mobile to enhance a picture
- To learn what a shadow box is

Materials:
- Box covers (Your students should bring their own. It should not be larger than 12″ x 18″. Shoe box covers work well.)
- Blue construction paper, 12″ x 18″
- White mimeograph paper
- Blue thread
- Masking tape
- Glue
- Toothpicks
- Tempera paint
- Brushes
- Water containers
- Scissors
- Pencils

LESSON 76

Discussion: • This project should be done on a snowy day. Have your students look out the window and describe how the snow looks as it softly piles on objects.

Define a mobile (a sculpture which has movement and is suspended in the air). Define a shadow box (a scene painted and set in a box. It is sometimes three dimensional.).

Procedure: • Direct each of your students to:
Lay the box top on the blue construction paper and trace around it.

Cut out the paper just inside the line. Place the paper inside the cover to be sure it fits and then remove it.

Paint the sides of the cover both inside and out with blue tempera paint and set it aside to dry.

Paint a snowy day picture on the blue construction paper with tempera paints and set it aside to dry.

Glue the picture inside the cover to make a shadow box picture.

Cut 8 lengths of thread. These should be long enough to cover the front of the cover, extend over one side, and be attached to the back.

Pull the threads taut and fasten all ends to the desk with small pieces of masking tape.

Fold the mimeograph paper in quarters.

Cut out small circles through the four thicknesses for snowflakes.

Slide the circles under the threads. Do not place them closer together than one inch, and vary the amount of space between them. (Snowflakes fall randomly.)

Squeeze a few drops of glue on to a scrap of paper.

Use a toothpick and place a tiny dot of glue on the thread over each circle.

Cover each circle with another circle; the same dot of glue will sandwich both circles together and seal in the thread.

Cut the threads loose at one end.

Peel the masking tape at the other end from the desk, making sure the thread stays attached.

Attach the masking tape to the back of the cover leaving the snowflake threads hanging over the picture.

Follow the same procedure with all the threads.

Cut off any thread that is extending below the last snowflake on the string.

Illustrations: • Snowy paper weights
These are another example of movement in a 3-D scene.

Suggestion: • Raindrops work equally as well as snowflakes.

LESSON 77
OVERLAPPING PAPER PICTURE

Objective:
- To stimulate awareness of depth perception

Materials:
- Construction paper, all colors
- Scissors
- Glue

Discussion:
- Look out the window. From what you can see, discuss objects that are in front of others. For example:

  A tree has a cloud behind it.
  Houses have other houses behind them.

  Your students should discover overlapping (the object in front covers up part of the object behind). Show your students examples from this book or examples you have made.

Procedure:
- Direct each of your students to:

  Decide on a theme for the picture. Some suggestions are: buildings in a city, crowds, cars on a street, and a house or a flower garden behind a picket fence.

  Draw each complete object on the construction paper.

  Cut out all the objects.

  Glue the paper objects on a background paper realistically. This will require overlapping; i.e., a tree in front of a house will be glued over part of the house.

Illustration:
- Magazine pictures that show overlapping or a great deal of depth would further reinforce this concept as seen in the everyday world.

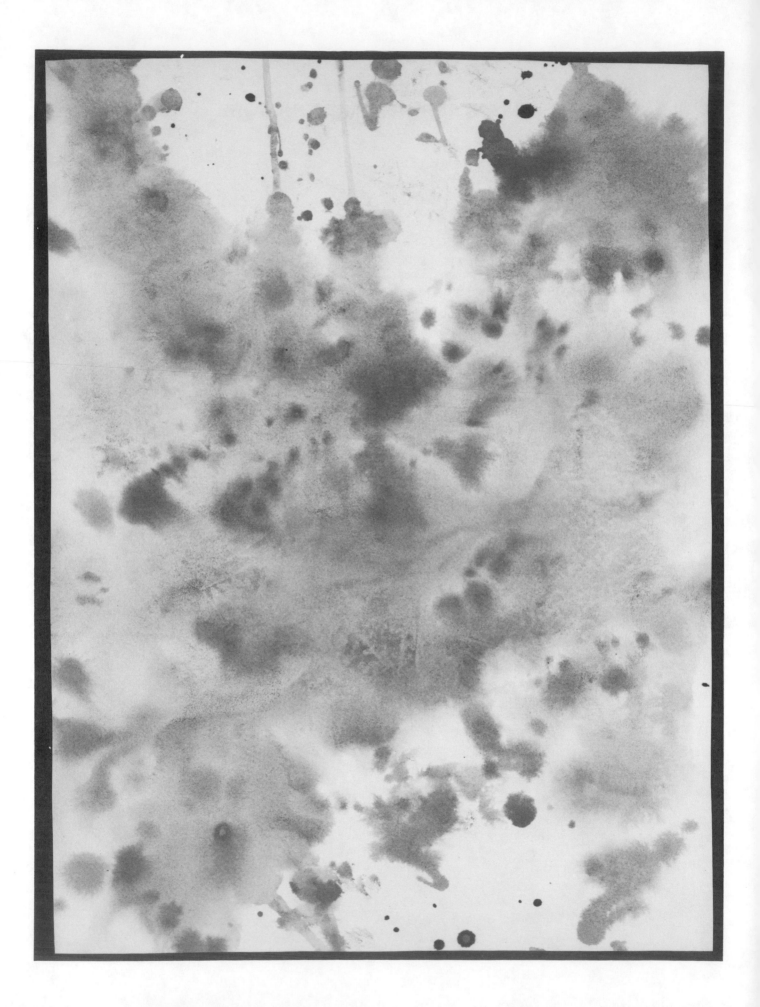

LESSON 78
WATERCOLORS

Objective:
- To explore the medium
- To discover color mixing

Materials:
- White construction paper
- Watercolor paint boxes
- Water containers
- Large brushes
- Corrugated cardboard for drawing boards (the side of any average size grocery box)
- Pincher clothespins (to clip paper to drawing board)
- Paper towels
- Sponges

Discussion:
- Tell your students to put a drop or two of water in each color while you are explaining the project. This will soften the paints. Have them print their names on the backs of their papers. Demonstrate the use and care of watercolors:

   Dip the brush in water.

   Lay the brush on the watercolor square sideways, the back of the brush slightly raised.

   Roll the brush over the square so all sides get covered with color.

   Do not put the point of the brush straight down into the paint. This will cause the bristles to spread and ruin the brush.

   Every time you use a new color rinse the brush.

   Do not let the brush stand in the water container. Lay it in the box when not in use or it will develop a bend.

   Leave the paintbox clean. If any water is left in the paint square, roll the clean brush over the square to get rid of it.

   Leave your brush clean and pointed.

Procedure:
- Direct each of your students to:

   Wet the entire sheet of paper with a large brush or sponge.

   Load the brush fully with paint.

   Splash the paint on the damp paper. The brush may have to be shaken to get a light spatter.

   Follow the same procedure with other colors.

   Fill the entire paper with drops and splashes.

   Set the paper aside to dry.
- Your students should discover that colors expand and/or blend with another nearby color.
- Save these sheets for the next lesson.

Illustration:
- Brian Wildsmith, SQUIRRELS, (New York: Franklin Watts, Inc., 1974)

   The trees and backgrounds illustrate the random drop technique. All of the illustrations are done in watercolor which the students have just explored and should be able to discuss.

Caution:
- *This is a short project.*

LESSON 79
SILHOUETTES

Objective:
- To learn what a silhouette is
- To discover that a black silhouette against a soft, light background creates a dramatic effect

Materials:
- Black construction paper, 9" x 12"
- Newsprint, 9" x 12"
- Pencils
- Masking tape
- Scissors
- Glue
- Watercolor sheets class made in preceding lesson
- Pictures of birds and flowers for reference

Discussion:
- Define a silhouette (a picture in outline form with no detail. It is similar to a shadow.).

  Use your reference pictures to compare and discuss the overall forms of different birds and flowers.

Procedure:
- Direct each of your students to:

  Draw a bird or a flower on newsprint. The drawings should fill the paper. Tell your students they do not have to worry about details such as eyes or color because only the outline is important for a silhouette.

  Tape the picture on a sheet of black construction paper.

  Cut out the picture from both the newsprint and the black construction paper at the same time.

  Position the black silhouette on the watercolor sheet.

  Glue.

Illustration:
- Richard Lewis, IN A SPRING GARDEN, (New York: The Dial Press, 1974)

  This book combines silhouettes against unusual or simple backgrounds with Haiku poetry. This book beautifully demonstrates a relationship between art and poetry.

LESSON 80
PAPER WEAVING

Objective:
- To discover that variations in weaving can create unusual effects
- To learn about Op art

Materials:
- Black construction paper, 9" x 12"
- White construction paper, 9" x 12"
- Scissors
- Glue

Discussion:
- Talk about optical illusions. Ask your students to guess what Op (optical) art might be. (Op art creates the feeling of movement through lines and shapes.)

  Review the terms warp, weft, and loom.

  The *loom* is the thing you weave on.
  The *warp* is the lengthwise thread that is strung on the loom.
  The *weft* is the thread that is woven over and under the warp.

Procedure:
- Demonstrate the entire procedure before having your students work independently.

  Cut a loom from the black construction paper with curves that all move in the same direction. Stop about 1½" from the top.

  Cut curved weft strips one at a time from the white construction paper.

  Weave each weft strip right after it is cut.

  Weave to within 2" of the bottom.

  Cut a strip of black construction paper, 2" x 9".

  Seal the bottom of the weaving by gluing the strip across the bottom of the loom.

- Have your students do one weaving exactly as you have demonstrated.

- Let your students try a second weaving with a different set of curving lines to get a different Op art effect.

Illustration:
- Rene Parola, OPTICAL ART, THEORY AND PRACTICE (New York: Beekman House, 1969) pp. 82 - 86.

  This book illustrates wide variations in Op art weaving and drawing.

LESSON 81
VALENTINE MOBILE

Objective:
- To make a mobile
- To create a three-dimensional effect from flat shapes

Materials:
- Construction paper
- Scissors
- Pencils
- Mimeograph paper
- Thread (24" - 20" - 14" - 10")
- Popsicle sticks, two for each student
- Yarn

Discussion:
- Define three-dimensional shapes (things that can be seen from all sides). Define a mobile (an abstract sculpture with movement that is suspended in mid-air). Tell your students they are going to make a valentine mobile using three-dimensional hearts.

LESSON 81

Ask your students how you could put two hearts together to make one so that no matter which side you look at you'll see a heart. Demonstrate with two identical hearts. On the first heart, cut straight up from the point to the middle; on the second heart, cut straight down from the indent to the middle. Put the cut point on the cut indent and slide the hearts together.

Demonstrate how the hearts will be hung. Before you make your two hearts into one, take a thread and pull it through the heart's slit that goes from the point to the middle. See that the ends are even and tie a double knot as close to the indent as possible. Then knot the two threads at the end. The hearts can then be slipped together.

Procedure: • Direct each of your students to:

Glue two popsicle sticks together in the middle making a + and set them aside to dry.

Make four different sized heart patterns from the mimeograph paper, the largest about 4".

Put two contrasting pieces of construction paper together and trace your heart pattern on one.

Cut both pieces of paper at the same time to make two identical hearts.

Cut slits, tie thread, and make one three-dimensional heart.

Repeat the procedure for all four hearts. Color combinations can vary.

Attach yarn to the popsicle sticks for hanging. Put the yarn between two opposite openings of the popsicle sticks. Make the yarn ends equal in length and tie a single knot that touches the sticks. Turn the sticks over, bring the yarn up through the other two openings, and tie another single knot. This will balance the sticks evenly. Knot the two equal lengths at the end.

Slip the heart threads over the ends of the popsicle sticks and balance the mobile.

Secure the threads with a drop of glue.

Suggestion: • Hearts may be decorated before making them three-dimensional.

Exemplar: • Alexander Calder, "Lobster Trap and Fish Tail", in H. W. Janson, HISTORY OF ART, (Englewood Cliffs, N.J.: Prentice-Hall, Inc., 1968) p. 537.

Tell your students that artists have worked to create motion in various ways and Calder was the first to ever create sculptures that really moved.

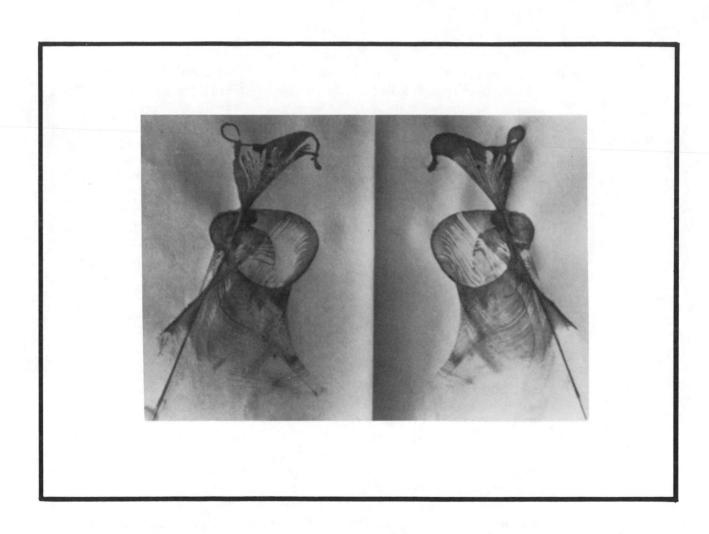

LESSON 82
STRING PAINTING — ACCIDENTAL DESIGN

Objective:
- To stretch the imagination
- To have art be the stimulus for a creative writing experience

Materials:
- Construction paper, 9″ x 12″
- String or yarn
- Tempera paint
- Paper towels

Discussion:
- Draw several scribbles on the blackboard. As each is drawn, your students should be urged to tell what they 'see' in it. Stress that imagination is the part of us that helps us to 'see' things in many different ways.

Procedure:
- Direct each of your students to:

    Fold the construction paper in half and then reopen it.

    Dip the yarn or the string into the tempera paint.

    Hold the string above the container and allow the excess paint to drip off.

    Arrange the string on one half of the paper leaving one end of the string extended over an edge.

    Refold the other half of the paper over the string.

    Rub a hand gently over the paper.

    Place a hand on the paper with a slight pressure and pull the string out by its end.

    Open the paper and allow the design to dry.

- While the paper is drying, your students should write paragraphs telling what they see in their designs.

- Staple the stories to the bottom of the design papers and display.

Illustration:
- Neil Appelbaum, IS THERE A HOLE IN YOUR HEAD?, (Katonah, New York: Young Reader's Press, Inc., 1963)

    This book whimsically illustrates how imagination can help us see many things in one abstract shape.

LESSON 83
FIGURE DRAWING

Objective: •   To become aware of the human figure, its characteristics and proportions

Materials: •   Drawing paper or newsprint
       •   Black magic markers or black crayons
       •   Pencils

Discussion: •   Work with a model - an adult or student volunteer. Some students love to pose; some hate it and should not be forced. A prop helps the model; for example, a guitar, a ball, or a chair.

Encourage your students to observe the model carefully. Ask questions such as the following:

What is the model doing?

How big is the head in comparison to the body?

How big are the hands?

     Put your hand over your face.

     Are you surprised at how much it covers?

If the model's arms were hanging straight down, where would the fingers touch?

Are the feet as big as the hands?

How high do the arms reach above the head?

Procedure: •   Direct each of your students to:

Look carefully at the model.

Compare the relationships of one part of the body to the other before putting it on paper; for example; how much wider are the shoulders than the head?

Sketch the figure lightly with pencil beginning at the top of the paper with the head.

Draw the figure large enough to fill the page.

Trace over the pencil lines with magic marker.

Try to get a true figure, but not necessarily a true likeness.

       •   Do not write the model's name on the paper.

Exemplar: •   Alice Elizabeth Chase, FAMOUS PAINTINGS, (New York: Platt and Munk, 1962) pp. 8-13.

Many artists have painted children. Your students should be able to see style differences in the portraits pictured here. The text is helpful for your explanations.

Suggestion: •   A second, full color drawing could be made using crayons or pastels.

LESSON 84
AN EXPLOSION IN A PAINT FACTORY — PAINTING

Objective:
- To stimulate the imagination
- To paint an imaginary picture

Materials:
- White drawing paper, 12″ x 18″
- Pencils
- Tempera paint
- Brushes
- Water containers

Discussion:
- Ask your students what a factory looks like. Ask them what color paints a paint company would make. Discuss what an explosion is. Consider what happens to the building. How high would things fly into the air? Would there be a fire? Tell them they are going to paint a picture of an explosion in a paint factory.

Procedure:
- Direct each of your students to:

  Sketch the picture in pencil on the drawing paper.

  Make the drawing large enough to fill the paper.

  Paint with tempera.

Exemplars:
- Wassily Kandinsky, "Sketch I for Composition VII," in H. W. Janson HISTORY OF ART, (Englewood Cliffs, N.J.: Prentice-Hall, Inc., 1968) p. 515.

  The explosive color in this painting, as well as its abstract quality make it a good example for your students after this assignment.

- Jackson Pollock, Detail of "One", H. W. Janson HISTORY OF ART, (Englewood Cliffs, N.J.: Prentice-Hall, Inc., 1968) p. 535.

  This oil painting is by one of America's outstanding contemporary artists. His abstract style is reminiscent of the project your students have just finished.

LESSON 85
WIRE SCULPTURE

Objective:
- To review what a sculpture is
- To create a wire sculpture

Materials:
- Small block of scrap wood with a nail pounded in the center so that the nail extends up about 3/4" to 1"
- Scissors
- Black tempera paint
- Brushes
- Colored, plastic coated wire cut in 2' lengths. (This can be purchased at a hardware store.)

Discussion:
- Review the definition of a sculpture (a complete three-dimensional figure or design; it is something you can look at from all sides. A statue is a sculpture.). Tell your students they are going to make a sculpture with wire. They will use wire like a pencil line to draw their sculpture. Ask them what they think would be a good subject for a sculpture. (Animals and flowers are the two easiest projects for this level, but do not discourage them from trying other ideas.)

  Demonstrate how to handle wire:

    Wire is easily bent, shaped and cut; it handles much like pipe cleaners.

    Wire can be looped and twisted around a supporting wire.

    Added lengths of wire can be twisted on at any point.

    Different shapes can be made and attached to the main form by twisting.

    Wire will not sag; it stays the way it is bent.

Procedure:
- Direct each of your students to:

    Take a piece of wire and a wooden base.

    Decide on a figure for the sculpture.

    Wind one end of the wire tightly around the nail two or three times to anchor it.

    Form the sculpture using the wire techniques that were demonstrated.

    Paint the base with black tempera paint when the sculpture is finished. Place a dot of black paint on the nail head to camouflage it.

Exemplar:
- Alexander Calder, "Cow" in Shirley Glubok, THE ART OF AMERICA IN THE EARLY TWENTIETH CENTURY, (New York: Macmillan Publishing Co., Inc., 1974)

    This is a wire sculpture.

Suggestion:
- Wire can often be acquired from the telephone company. They do recycle wire, but managers will generally give used wire to a school as a matter of public relations.

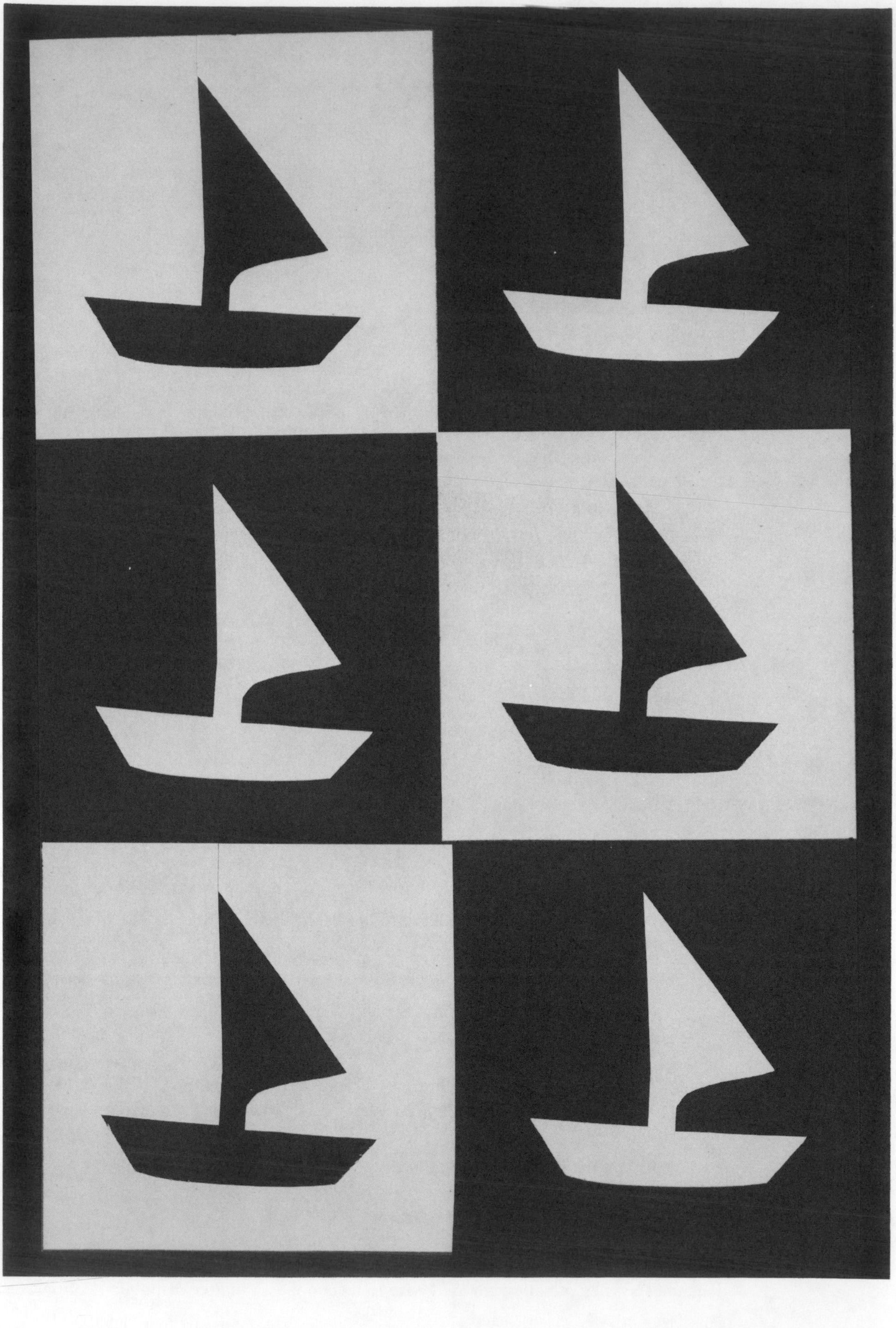

LESSON 86
POSITIVE—NEGATIVE REPEAT PATTERN

Objective:
- To create a repeat pattern
- To work with a positive/negative design

Materials:
- Dark construction paper, 12″ x 18″
- Light construction paper, 6″ x 6″ (each student needs 3)
- Newsprint, 6″ x 6″
- Pencils
- Scissors
- Glue

Discussion:
- Ask your students to define a repeat pattern (one that occurs over and over and over). Tell them they will be making repeat patterns using opposites. Have your students suggest as many opposite word pairs as they can. Show your students an example of a silhouette form cut from a 6″ paper square. Ask them why the shape and the leftover square minus the shape can be considered opposites. Tell your students the shape is a silhouette (a picture in outline form with no detail, similar to a shadow).

Procedure:
- Demonstrate the entire procedure before having your students work independently.

  Decide on a silhouette form.

  Draw practice sketches on the newsprint until you are satisfied with the outline.

  Cut out the newsprint silhouette.

  Lay the silhouette on the center of the 6″ construction paper square and trace around it.

  Cut straight in from the edge and then around the traced shape. Both the shape and the leftover 'frame' must be used, so care must be taken to cut accurately.

  Repeat with two other 6″ squares.

  Arrange the repeat pattern on 12″ x 18″ background paper; the paper may be placed horizontally or vertically.

  Glue.

- Display the finished patterns on the bulletin board.

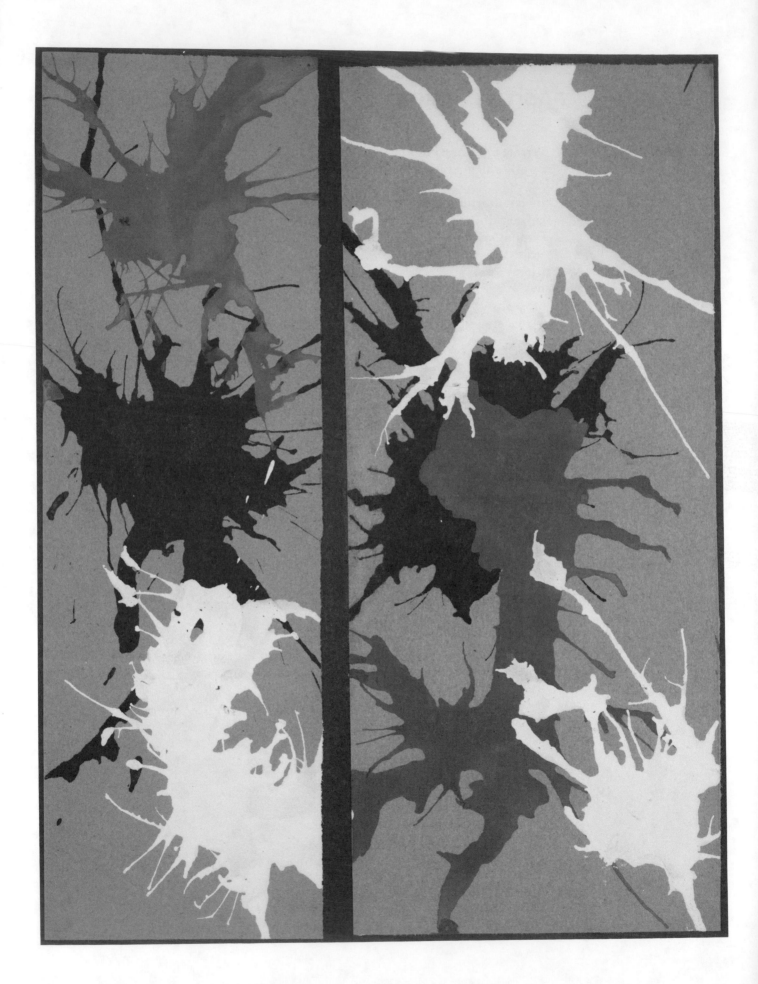

LESSON 87
ABSTRACT FLOWERS — ACCIDENTAL DESIGN

Objective: • To discover how controlled, accidental design can result in a pleasing abstraction

Materials:
- Pastel construction paper, 6" x 16"
- Dark construction paper, 8" x 18"
- Thin tempera paints, several colors plus black
- Plastic bowls (to hold tempera paint)
- Spoons
- Straws

Discussion: • Ask your students what abstract art is (something you look at that reminds you of the color, shape, or feel of a real object even though it doesn't look exactly like that object).

Procedure: • Direct each of your students to:

Select two colors of tempera paint as well as black.

Spoon a small amount of the black tempera paint on to the pastel paper.

Blow the paint in all directions with a straw.

Allow the paint to partially dry.

Spoon a small amount of a second color of tempera paint on to the paper, placing it in a different area than the black.

Blow the paint in all directions with a straw, and again allow the paint to dry. Some of the paint will overlap the black.

Spoon a small amount of a third color on to the paper, placing it in a new area, and repeat the above procedure.

Mount the finished work with glue on the 8" x 18" dark construction paper.

Illustration: • Japanese prints

Point out to your students that the brush strokes typical of Japanese watercolors resemble the blown lines of their designs.

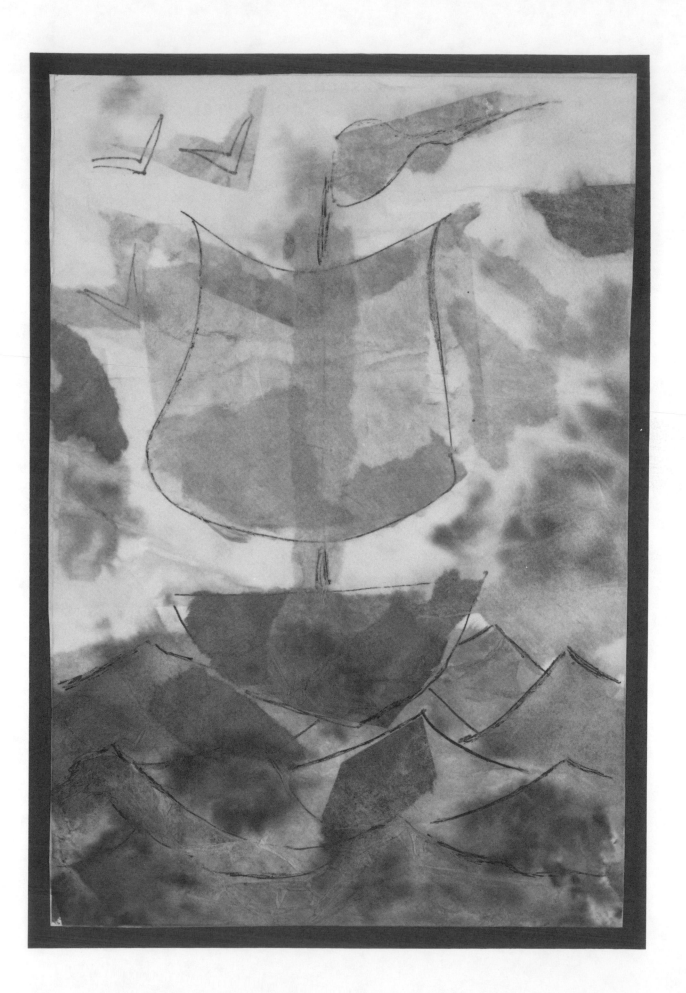

LESSON 88
TISSUE PAPER COLLAGE

Objective:
- To create a collage
- To make a line drawing

Materials:
- White drawing paper, 9″ x 12″
- Black permanent magic markers
- Tissue paper scraps, varied colors
- Paint brushes
- Containers for glue mixture
- White glue mixed half and half with water

Discussion:
- Talk about spring and all the things that distinguish it from winter, summer, and fall. A short walk to look for signs of spring is valuable.

  Discuss color mixing. Have your students tell how to make new colors from the primary colors (red, yellow, and blue). Write the combinations on the blackboard: red + blue = purple; blue + yellow = green; red + yellow = orange. Hold two colors of tissue paper up to a window and demonstrate making new colors by overlapping.

Procedure:
- Direct each of your students to:

  Make a line drawing of spring on the white paper using a permanent magic marker.

  Tear small pieces of tissue paper (1″ to 2″).

  Paint the drawing with the glue mixture.

  Start the tissue paper collage with light colored paper as it is hard to change dark colors by overlapping.

  Lay the desired colors of tissue paper on the wet glue; pieces should overlap.

  Paint over the tissue paper with the glue mixture. The tissue paper dye will run slightly. This does not hurt the overall effect.

  Set the finished collage aside to dry.

- If the tissue paper sticks out over the edge of the drawing paper it can be trimmed when the picture is dry.

LESSON 89
BURLAP STITCHERY

Objective:
- To create an original stitchery

Materials:
- Burlap, precut into 12″ x 12″ pieces, edges enclosed in masking tape to prevent raveling
- Burlap, miscellaneous sizes for students to practice stitches on
- Embroidery hoops, approximately 10″ in diameter
- Blunt end darning needles, placed in small squares of construction paper to prevent rolling
- Scissors
- Yarn, a variety of colors
- Reference book showing embroidery stitches, for your use

Discussion:
- Review the definition of a stitchery (a design or picture made by sewing). Distribute the yarn, hoops, needles and practice burlap pieces to your students. Demonstrate threading a needle and knotting the end of the yarn so that it won't pull through the material. *Stress the safe use of needles.*

  Review the running, satin, star, split, and whipped stitches. Your students learned these in level two. Have your students make a sample of each stitch on the burlap after your demonstration.

  Demonstrate the new stitches: blanket, chain, and lazy daisy. Have your students practice each.

  Tell your students they are going to make a flower garden stitchery. Ask what stitches they might use for different parts of their picture; for example, the blanket stitch for grass, and the lazy daisy or the satin stitch for flowers.

Procedure:
- Direct each of your students to:

  Select the yarn colors they want to work with.

  Stitch their flower garden free hand.

- Details such as a sun, butterflies, birds, or bugs may be included.

Suggestion:
- You may want to have parent volunteers present for this project. Having one adult work with a small group of four or five students would eliminate problems.

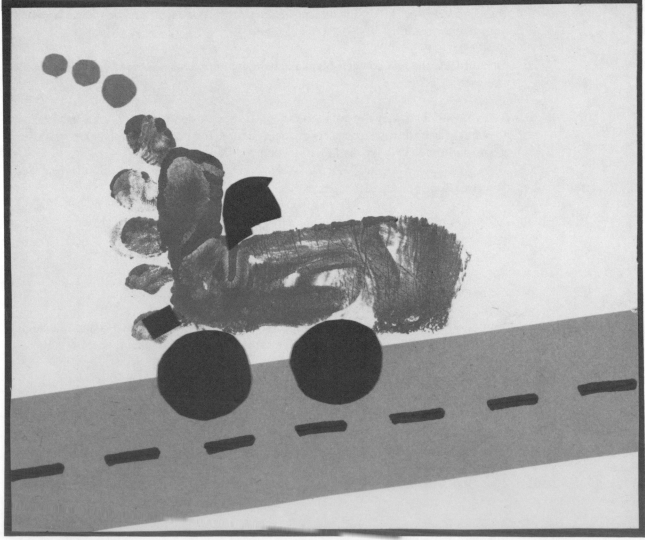

LESSON 90
FOOTPRINTING — IMAGINATION

Objective:
- To discover a new form of printing
- To stretch the imagination

Materials:
- White drawing paper, 9″ x 12″
- Tempera paint in shallow, footsized containers
- Paper towels, water, and soap for cleanup
- Construction paper, miscellaneous paper scraps

Discussion:
- Talk about the process of fingerprinting as a means of identifying people. Tell your students that a footprint was made at the hospital when they were born to identify them. Tell them they are going to make footprints.

  Review the definition of printing (stamping or pressing an object covered with paint on to a paper. When lifted off, the object leaves a print.).

Procedure:
- Direct each of your students to:

  Remove the right or the left shoe; only one foot need be bare.

  Step in the paint.

  Place the foot on the paper and then lift if off to reveal a footprint.

  Wash and dry the foot while the paint dries.

  Look at the print from all angles to 'see' a picture in the print.

  Cut paper details from the construction paper scraps and glue to the print to create a picture.

Illustration:
- Polly Chase Boyden, "Mud", in May Hill Arbuthnot, TIME FOR POETRY, (New York: Scott, Foresman and Co., 1952) p. 146.

  Reading this poem aloud to your students emphasizes the feel of the paint on their feet and shows fun in the art form of poetry.

GLOSSARY

Abstract art — a visual interpretation that expresses the essence of a figure, object, or place with little regard for its natural appearance.

Asymmetric — a balance in art where each side of a composition has varied or different parts. Also called informal balance.

Bas-relief — a sculpture which is not free standing; one side is flat, or attached to a surface. The design or figure is carved so it extends outward on the other side.

Batik — a picture on fabric created by sealing some areas with wax and dying the others.

Bisque — unglazed pottery after first firing.

Collage — a composition made by gluing various materials to a background.

Color harmonies: **Complimentary** — colors opposite each other on the color wheel.

Analogous — colors next to each other on the color wheel.

Monochromatic — varied shades of one color.

Colors: Primary — red, yellow and blue. The colors from which all other colors are created.

Secondary — orange, green, purple. The colors made from two primary colors.

Terciary — colors made from mixing a primary and a secondary color. The primary color is always the first named colored of a terciary hue.

Composition — arrangement of all parts of a picture or design into a pleasing, complete whole.

Contour line — a line that follows the outline of a shape.

Cool colors — green, blue, violet. Colors associated with water, sky and plants.

Design — a pleasing arrangement of one or more of the elements of art.

Elements of art — color, line, shape, form, texture, and balance.

Emphasis — an area of special importance created by some dramatic use of size, color, texture of shape.

Exemplar — an example of fine art. It must be authenticated by an authority or proven by time.

Fixatif — a commercial spray, usually plastic, to protect easily smudged works of art.

Focal point — the dominant point of interest that draws the viewers eye.

Form — a three dimensional shape.

Found objects — any objects 'found' on a walk or in a certain place. They can be used for printing or in an art composition.

Frottage — the design created by making a rubbing of a raised surface.

Glaze — the finished surface of ceramics.

Greenware — ceramics that are leather hard, but not fired.

Hatching — lines drawn at a slant to build up areas of darkness. Also, crosshatching, where lines are slanted across each other for the same purpose.

Horizon line — the imaginary line where sky and earth meet.

Hue — color.

Illustration — an example that further develops or clarifies a technique or an idea for a student.

Intaglio — a design cut into, or engraved below, the surface.

Intensity — the degree of brightness or dullness.

Kiln — an oven for firing ceramics.

Line — an element of art made by moving a point.

Mass — a large area in a composition: it can be created by color, shape or texture.

Mat board — a heavy cardboard for mounting pictures.

Medium — a particular material used in an art project.

Mobile — a sculpture that has movement and is suspended in mid air.

Modelling — using clay to form a three-dimensional structure.

Monoprint — a single print made by laying a paper on a fingerpainting (or oil or ink) smoothing it gently, and lifting it off, transferring the picture to the paper.

Mosaic — a picture formed by using small pieces of colored glass, tile, or paper.

Motif — dominant theme or feature of a composition.

Mural — a long wall decoration.

Paper-mache — torn paper strips soaked in a paste solution.

Pastels — colored chalk.

Perspective — distance represented on a flat surface.

Positive — Negative — opposite or reversed (mirrored) images.

Proportions — the relation of each part to the other.

Relief — sculpture, not free standing, that is attached to something.

Rhythm — an ordered movement in art created by repetition of some art element.

Shade — color plus black. Darker than pure pigment.

Slip — clay mixed with water to consistency of cream and used to fasten pieces of clay together.

Stained glass — colored glass held together by leading or copper foil.

Symmetric — a balance in art where each side of a composition has identical parts. Also called formal balance.

Tactile — refers to the sense of touch.

Tempra — an opaque, water soluable paint.

Texture — the actual or visual feel of a surface.

Tint — color plus white. Lighter than pure pigment.

Value — the lightness or darkness of a color.

Vanishing point — in perspective drawings, the point at which all lines disappear.

Warm colors — red, orange and brown. Colors usually associated with fire, sun and earth.